7/7/2025

# Phrasal Verbs, Idioms, and Prepositions for Better Writing and Competitive Exam Preparation

*With Question Sets, Reference & Answers*

Copyright © 2024 Mr. Peter
All rights reserved.

First Edition- May 2024

Last Updated: 07-07-2025

This book has been published with efforts to ensure error-free content with the author's consent. No part may be reproduced without written permission from the author, except for the lines, words, or phrases used for educational purposes. The Publisher and Author do not guarantee the accuracy or reliability of the information. If printing or binding defects exist, the Publisher will replace the defective copy when available.

The work is published in association with Amazon, Notion Press, and Google, ensuring its availability in various formats and markets worldwide.

https://kdp.amazon.com/en_US/ & https://notionpress.com/

# DEDICATION

The book is dedicated to all my friends, students, and colleagues whose inspiration and cooperation made it possible for you to hold this book in your hand.

## *Preface*

*I am honored to write the preface for this book by Mr. Peter. He is a prominent author of educational books for high school students and a respected writer of fiction, poetry, and short stories. This book, as the title suggests, includes a list of Phrasal Verbs (including question sets for practice) and over 372 selected idioms with sentences, as well as the conjugation of Prepositions with Verbs, Nouns, Adjectives, and Participles. I believe these resources will be helpful for students in improving their speaking, writing, and performance in competitive exams, where these sections are crucial for scoring marks, especially since English is often a second language for students from many countries.*

*Sd/*
*Dr. Moklesur Rahaman,*
*Esteemed Educator in India*

# CONTENTS

*Chapters* *Pages*

# Phrasal Verbs: Learn How They Are Formed

## Definition of Phrasal Verbs

1. **Read the bold words and study their meanings:**
    - **Get:** a verb meaning ***'****to receive something'*;
    - **By:** a preposition to denote *'the method of doing something'*;
    - **Get by:** a phrasal verb that means **'live with difficulty.'**

A **phrasal verb** is a phrase formed by ***a verb followed by an adverb, a preposition, or both***. Together, the two or three words function as a single unit of verb, which means something different from the individual words.

## How They Are Formed

As said, a Phrasal Verb is formed by ***a verb followed by an adverb, a preposition, or both.*** Thus, a phrasal verb is a phrase of two or three words. Read some examples of how they are formed:

**A. Verb + Adverb = Phrasal Verbs**

| ***Verb*** | ***Adverb*** | ***Phrasal Verbs*** | ***Meanings*** |
|---|---|---|---|
| Bear | Down | Bear down | He was determined to ***bear down*** all obstacles. (to defeat) |
| Break | Away | Break away | The prisoner ***broke away*** from captivity. (escaped) |
| Bring | Out | Bring out | My first novel was ***brought out*** in 2020 during the lockdown. (published) |
| Call | Out | Call out | He was ***called out*** for an urgent task. (summoned) |
| Go | Up | Go up | The price of essential commodities is ***going up***. (increasing) |
| Set | Down | Set down | The police ***set down*** the complaint. (Recorded) |
| Run | Over | Run over | A poor dog was ***run over*** by the car. (knocked down) |
| Turn | Aside | Turn aside | We should not ***turn aside*** from the path of honesty. (deviate) |

**B. Verb + Prepositions = Phrasal Verbs**

| ***Verb*** | ***Preposition*** | ***Phrasal Verbs*** | ***Meanings*** |
|---|---|---|---|
| Bring | On | Bring on | The damp weather has ***brought on*** |

| | | | |
|---|---|---|---|
| | | | his illness. (led to) |
| Call | At | Call at | We ***called*** him ***at*** his house. (met) |
| Carry | On | Carry on | ***Carry on*** the project till it is finished. (continue) |
| Laugh | At | Laugh at | Your friends may ***laugh at*** you. Still, you move on. (mock at/show negligence) |
| Look | After | Look after | Parents ***look after*** their children to the utmost end. (take care of) |
| Put | On | Put on | You don't need to ***put on*** you are an honest man. (take disguise) |
| Run | At | Run at | The tiger ***ran at*** the deer. (chased) |
| Set | Up | Set up | I ***set up*** my White Home in June 2020. (founded) |

**C. Verb + Adverb + Prepositions = Phrasal Verbs**

| ***Verb*** | ***Adverb*** | ***Prepositions*** | ***Phrasal Verbs*** | ***Meanings*** |
|---|---|---|---|---|
| Look | Down | Upon | Look down upon | We should not ***look down upon*** the poor. (hate/neglect) |
| Set | Out + for | - | Set out for | They ***set out for*** the picnic spot early in the morning. (started) |
| Do | Away | With | Do away with | The young actress tried to ***do away with*** herself. (commit suicide) |
| Fall | -- | In + with | Fall in with | The principal ***fell in with*** the decision of the guardian committee. (agreed/gave consent) |

# Let's Practice in Question Set

(When you already know something about them):

## 1 to 50 Sets of Questions

**Instruction: Replace** *the* **bold** *or* **Italic words** in the sentences *with suitable* **phrasal verbs** from the box given for each set. You may have to change the forms of verbs as necessary (as per Tense, Voice, Subject-Verb Agreement). There is no extra phrasal verb in the lists:

**Set 1:**

| a. set in | b. put up with | c. lay-up | d. give up |
|---|---|---|---|

c, a, b, d

1) A certain ailment could **confine** a patient to bed for three days.
2) This year, in June, the monsoon **began**.
3) I cannot **tolerate** such rude behavior.
4) We should **abolish** bad habits.

**Set 2:**

| a. hand in | b. give in | c. come across | d. turn down |
|---|---|---|---|

c, d, b, a

5) Rabi **met** his friend in the park.
6) His proposal was **rejected**.
7) The enemy **surrendered** without a fight.
8) He **offered** the marriage proposal.

**Set 3:**

| a. call up | b. come round | c. look into | d. make out |
|---|---|---|---|

b, c, d, a

9) The child was **cured** in a month.
10) The police **investigated** the case.
11) Puja could **understand** what her sister said.
12) The old man could not **remember** his childhood experiences.

**Set 4:**

| a. look down upon | b. take after | c. set up | d. bring out |
|---|---|---|---|

b, d, a, c

13) The child ***resembles*** his grandmother.
14) They ***published*** a magazine recently.
15) My mother taught me not to ***disrespect*** anyone.
16) A new university was ***built*** at Coochbehar.

**Set 5:**

| a. Let it down | b. Stand against | c. Write down | d. Knock (sb) up |
|---|---|---|---|

**C, a, b, d**

17) ***Record*** your name and address on a piece of paper.
18) The machine won't ***fail to support***.
19) All the members of the staff committee ***opposed*** the principal's decision.
20) Please ***wake*** me ***up*** at five O'clock.

**Set 6:**

| a. Stand aside | b. Let (sb) in | c. Knock out | d. Write out |
|---|---|---|---|

**D, b, a, c**

21) Please ***write*** your name and address ***in full***.

22) What ***made*** her ***get involved in*** the situation?
23) Please ***give a place*** for the chairman to pass.
24) Mary Kom ***defeated*** her opponent in the next two rounds.

**Set 7:**

| a. Knock off | b. Write up | c. Stand aside | d. Let (sb) off |
|---|---|---|---|

**B, d, c, a**

25) Rahaman must ***write some lines praising*** my published books.
26) She was ***released*** with a warning.
27) He ***withdrew his name*** from the contest.
28) The shopkeeper will ***deduct*** a thousand rupees if you want to buy all Peter's books.

**Set 8:**

| a. Work in | b. Stand at | c. Let out | d. Keep up with |
|---|---|---|---|

**A, c, b, d**

29) The water has ***penetrated*** all around the packing box.
30) **Suddenly,** she **started** a scream of terror. (*Begin with:* She …)
31) The total contribution so far **is equal to** Rs. 10,000.
32) You must ***adjust to*** the changing world.

**Set 9:**

| a. Work off | b. Knock up | c. Stand by | d. Keep to |
|---|---|---|---|

**A, c, d, b**

33) Unless you ***get rid of*** excess fat, you will fall ill.
34) He will always ***support*** me.
35) You should always ***adhere to*** your principles.
36) He was ***exhausted*** after five hours of work.

**Set 10:**

| a. Keep on | b. Standoff | c. Work out | d. Knockdown |
|---|---|---|---|

**C, b, a, d**

37) I still cannot ***solve*** the sum.
38) I was merely a ***silent onlooker*** when they fought.
39) **Continue**. You must reach your goal.
40) He was ***hit*** by a taxi.

**Set 11:**

| a. Stand for | b. Work up | c. Go aside | d. Keep down |
|---|---|---|---|

**B, a, d, c**

41) The mob was ***excited*** by his fiery speech.
42) White ***symbolizes*** purity, and the letter 'L' symbolizes 'Learning.'
43) You must ***suppress*** your anger.
44) Don't ***deviate*** from the path of virtue.

**Set 12:**

| a. Stand-in | b. Go at | c. Keep back | d. Hold with |
|---|---|---|---|

**A, d, c, b**

45) The hero is absent; you are asked to ***be a substitute*** for him.
46) They ***agreed with*** us in this matter.
47) I never ***concealed*** anything from my lover.
48) The two brothers ***attack*** each other at the slightest provocation.

**Set 13:**

| a. Go away | b. Hold out | c. Stand in with | d. Tell against |
|---|---|---|---|

**D, c, b, a**

49) The evidence ***proved*** the accused ***guilty***.
50) This is a pretty big amount; let me ***share (expenditure) with*** you.
51) She always ***extended*** her helping hands to the known and the unknown.
52) The beggar has ***left*** with all his belongings.

**Set 14:**

| a. Go beyond | b. Tell upon | c. take off | d. Hold on |
|---|---|---|---|

**C, d, a, b**

53) I ***withdrew*** my name from the debate.
54) Please ***wait*** for a minute.
55) You should not ***cross*** your ***limits***.
56) Smoking started to ***affect*** his health.

**Set 15:**

| a. Hold in | b. Go down | c. Take back | d. Stand out |
|---|---|---|---|

**D, a, b, c**

57) Her performance ***was prominent*** from the rest.
58) **Check** your temper. None here to bear with.
59) The price of butter has been ***reduced***.
60) I will not ***withdraw*** my words.

**Set 16:**

| a. Take (sb) for | b. Holdback | c. Stand to | d. Go for |
|---|---|---|---|

**C, b, d, a**

61) We should ***stick to*** our principles.
62) Truth can never be ***concealed***.
63) Shall I ***call*** a doctor?
64) Everyone ***considered*** him an honest man.

**Set 17:**

| a. Turn against | b. Stand up for | c. Holdback | d. Go off |
|---|---|---|---|

**A, b, c, d**

65) I do not know why he ***became hostile to*** me.
66) They are determined to ***vindicate*** ***(fight for)*** their rights.
67) **Hide** your weakness from your dear ones, and you are safe.
68) The bomb ***exploded,*** and many people were injured.

**Set 18:**

| a. Grow up | b. Hang about | c. Lookup | d. Go out |
|---|---|---|---|

**D, c, b, a**

69) The lamp has ***extinguished*** after twelve minutes.
70) After a dull period, Peter's business is ***improving***.
71) The little child ***remains close to*** his father.
72) **Stop acting like a child**. Why cry over love and love? It is a meaningless game on thy earth!

**Set 19:**

| a. Lookup | b. Go through | c. Take in | d. Hang on |
|---|---|---|---|

**B, c, a, d**

73) I shall ***examine*** the papers ***fully***.
74) I was ***cheated*** by the grocer.
75) ***Find out*** the nearest meaning of the word in the dictionary.
76) Would you please ***wait*** a minute?

**Set 20:**

| a. Go with | b. Look to /oil in | c. Take in | d. Hang out |
|---|---|---|---|

**A, c, b, d**

77) I ***agree with*** you on this matter.
78) We shall ***admit*** 100 students this year.
79) **Attend to** your affairs.
80) People ***displayed*** flags to welcome their leader.

**Set 21:**

| a. Hangover | b. Take off | c. Go after | d. Look through |
|---|---|---|---|

**C, b, d, a**

81) The soldiers ***chased*** the enemy.
82) The boy ***removed*** his shoes after returning from school.
83) Please ***carefully examine*** the letter and say where the mistakes are.
84) Do not ***bend down*** the open balcony.

**Set 22:**

| a. Take off | b. Turn away | c. Look over | d. Go against |
|---|---|---|---|

**B, d, a, c**

85) ***Dismiss*** the idea from your mind.
86) The police will ***oppose*** thc public interest.
87) Do not ***mimic*** a lame man.
88) The authority ***examined*** his application and finally sanctioned his two-month leave.

**Set 23:**

| a. Take off | b. Hangover | c. Look out for | d. Stare at |
|---|---|---|---|

**A, c, b, d**

89) The plane will ***start flying*** at 7 a.m.
90) The eagle is ***searching for*** prey.

91) The meeting has been ***postponed***.
92) The little boy is ***looking at*** us ***fixedly***.

**Set 24:**

| a. Look out for | b. Take off | c. Set aside | d. Hang up |
|---|---|---|---|

**B, a, d, c**

93) ***Remove*** your hands from my shoulders.
94) The police are ***trying to find*** the criminal.
95) A notice was ***put up*** on the wall.
96) The High Court ***canceled*** the judgment of the lower court.

**Set 25:**

| a. Give away | b. Take on | c. Set by | d. Look upon |
|---|---|---|---|

**C, b, d, a**

97) The beggar ***saved*** a huge amount of money by begging.
98) I decided to ***undertake*** an extra job for a better livelihood.
99) We ***regarded*** you only as our well-wishers, but we were wrong.
100) The chief guest, along with others, ***distributed*** the prizes on the school sports day.

**Set 26:**

| a. Lookup | b. Take out | c. Layout | d. Set forth |
|---|---|---|---|

**B, c, a, d**

101) ***Remove*** the aching tooth.
102) He ***expended*** his all in the business.
103) Pamela ***stood up*** and asked nothing.
104) Sophia ***started*** her journey last November.

**Set 27:**

| a. set off for | b. Lay on | c. Take over | d. Lookup |
|---|---|---|---|

**A, c, b, d**

105) Nicole ***left for*** Japan.
106) The new President will ***accept*** the charge of the government next month.
107) Taxes at the highest rate were ***imposed on*** the liquid.
108) Prices of all goods, including essential commodities, are ***rising.***

**Set 28:**

| a. Look up to | b. Take to | c. Lay off | d. Turn aside |
|---|---|---|---|

**C, a, d, b**

109) Some workers were ***suspended*** for their participation in the agitation.
110) I ***respect*** him as my elder brother.
111) We should not ***deviate*** from the path of honesty.
112) The young boy has been ***addicted to*** drinking recently.

**Set 29:**

| a. Bear with | b. Give away | c. Lay down | d. Take-up |
|---|---|---|---|

**D, c, b, a**

113) The car ***occupies*** too much space. We will replace it with a mini one.
114) Our freedom fighters ***sacrificed*** their lives for the cause of the country's liberation.
115) The soldier didn't ***reveal*** any secrets to our enemy.
116) I have to ***tolerate*** her during the difficult hours.

**Set 30:**

| a. Take (sth) up | b. Go abroad | c. Layby | d. Blow off |
|---|---|---|---|

**A, c, d, b**

117) I shall ***produce*** the matter with the principal, and let's see what can be done.
118) ***Save*** something for the future.
119) The chimneys ***emitted*** thick smoke.
120) Mr. Das often ***travels to foreign countries*** to attend business meetings.

**Set 31:**

| a. Backup | b. Blow up | c. Give out | d. Bring forth/in |
|---|---|---|---|

**C, b, a, d**

121) After a few days, our stock of rice will ***be exhausted***.
122) Opponent soldiers **exploded** the buildings.
123) He **supported** his friend's claim.
124) All trees **beget** (produce) new tender leaves during the rainy season.

**Set 32:**

| a. Give out | b. Blow up | c. Bring-in | d. Act up to |
|---|---|---|---|

**A, b, d, c**

125) The blast furnace is ***emitting*** a lot of heat.
126) You don't need to ***exaggerate*** your credits.
127) The machine does not ***work according to*** my expectations.
128) My business ***yields*** good income.

**Set 33:**

| a. Bring out | b. Bear away | c. Act upon | d. Give out |
|---|---|---|---|

**D, c, b, a**

129) The SBI Chairman ***declared*** a new interest in HBL and FDs.
130) The medicine ***affects*** the heart.
131) Preston ***won*** the prize for his talent.
132) My first book was ***published*** in 2013. It was a book of poems.

**Set 34:**

| a. Get around | b. Turn to | c. Bring out | d. Make out |
|---|---|---|---|

**C, b, d, a**

133) Proper training will ***reveal*** the best in him.
134) ***Pray to*** God, and He will save you.
135) I could not ***understand*** what he said.
136) The news of our President's death ***spread*** sooner than we hoped.

**Set 35:**

| a. Bring up | b. Getaway | c. Fall apart | d. Make out |
|---|---|---|---|

**A, d, b, c**

137) After the death of his father, he was ***reared*** by his mother.
138) **Prepare** a list of your books.
139) Thieves ***escaped*** with computer equipment worth three lakhs.
140) The glass **broke into pieces**.

**Set 36:**

| a. Fall away | b. Send down | c. Makeup | d. Get back |
|---|---|---|---|

**C, d, a, b**

141) Who will ***compensate*** for this loss?
142) When will you ***return*** from there?
143) The film star's fans ***left him, deserting him*** with the decline of his popularity.
144) We should ***send*** him ***to prison*** for his crime.

**Set 37:**

| a. Fall away | b. Call for | c. Makeup | d. Get by |
|---|---|---|---|

**C, d, a, b**

145) Two more boys will ***complete*** the team.
146) Most of the salaried men here ***manage to live*** on a small salary.
147) The black spots are yet to ***disappear*** from your face.
148) Please ***summon*** a doctor

**Set 38:**

| a. Makeup | b. Fall back | c. Get into | d. Pass away |
|---|---|---|---|

**A, c, b, d**

149) They ***decided*** to return.
150) He ***became involved in*** trouble with the police while still a student.
151) The enemy ***retreated*** with the advance of our troops.
152) The clouds have ***dispersed***.

**Set 39:**

| a. Pass away | b. Get off | c. Fall in | d. Make away with |
|---|---|---|---|

**D, b, c, a**

153) Farah ***destroyed*** her own life.
154) We **left** the meeting in the middle.
155) The new building **collapsed** within a year.
156) My old grandfather ***died*** last week.

**Set 40:**

| a. Fall off | b. Make off | c. Get out | d. Turn up |
|---|---|---|---|

**D, b, c, a**

157) A huge crowd ***appeared*** for the match.
158) The new bride ***escaped*** with all the ornaments from the house.
159) Few passengers were lucky enough to **escape** from the burning train.

160) Attendance in classes has ***decreased*** after the exams in schools.

**Set 41:**

| a. Pass by | b. Get over | c. Fall off | d. See off |
|---|---|---|---|

**B, c, a, d**

161) The old man could not ***overcome*** the shock of his son's death.
162) False friends **drop off** in misfortune.
163) We should not ***overlook /ignore*** our youngsters' faults.
164) I'll go to the station to ***bid farewell*** to my friend.

**Set 42:**

| a. Get through | b. Pass for | c. Fall on/upon | d. See in |
|---|---|---|---|

**A, c, b, d**

165) Please join us as soon as you **complete** your task.
166) Miscreants ***attacked*** them ***fiercely***.
167) He is ***regarded*** as a great scholar.
168) What did you ***find interesting about*** that black spot?

**Set 43:**

| a. Draw away | b. Fall out | c. Pass on | d. See in |
|---|---|---|---|

**B, c, d, a**

169) The boys ***began to quarrel*** with each other over the issue of the goal.
170) Let us ***proceed*** to another subject.
171) I don't know what she ***finds attractive about*** him.
172) His attention was ***diverted*** by the loud noise.

**Set 44:**

| a. Turn down | b. Draw out | c. See About | d. Fall to |
|---|---|---|---|

**D, a, c, b**

173) He **began** eating with greater gusto.
174) My claim was ***rejected***.
175) I will ***consider*** your proposal.
176) The girl is very shy and needs to be ***encouraged*** to talk.

**Set 45:**

| a. Draw out | b. Run up | c. Drop by | d. Do away with |
|---|---|---|---|

**A, b, c, d**

177) The professor ***prolonged*** the interview with Mr. Rahaman intentionally to test his patience for the job.
178) The Price of petrol ***increased*** to Rs 112. This is the third time within a month.
179) On his long journey, he **stopped** at every metropolitan city to visit his nearest ones.
180) The woman tried to ***commit suicide***.

**Set 46:**

| a. Come of | b. Put aside | c. Drop off | d. Run upon |
|---|---|---|---|

**D, c, b, a**

181) The cyclist ***collided with*** the lamp post and broke his thin helmet.
182) The number of friends ***reduces*** after one's marriage.
183) We all need to ***save*** some money for future use.
184) B. R. Ambedkar **was born into** a poor family.

**Set 47:**

| a. | Put away / Lay aside/ put aside | b. | Run into | c. | Come out | d. | Cry down |
|---|---|---|---|---|---|---|---|

**B, a, c, d**

185) He ***fell into*** debt.
186) ***Save*** enough money for your son's education.
187) The rain stopped, and the sun **appeared**.
188) Don't **decry /underestimate** his achievements. Think of what labor he gave, we couldn't.

**Set 48:**

| a. | Run into | b. | Come out | c. | Put away/Give up | d. | Cry down |
|---|---|---|---|---|---|---|---|

**A, c, b, d**

189) The bus ***collided with*** the railing of the bridge.
190) I tried a lot but had to ***abandon*** the idea of buying a car.
191) When is your next book **publishing**?
192) The helpless man **begged** the rioters for his life.

**Set 49:**

| a. | Cut out | b. | Runoff | c. | Cut in | d. | Put down |
|---|---|---|---|---|---|---|---|

**B, d, c, a**

193) The thief saw a policeman and ***fled***.
194) The rebellion can't be ***suppressed*** by the govt.
195) She kept on **interrupting** our conversation.
196) Maizie was **suitable** for this job.

**Set 50:**

| a. | Run on | b. | Put in | c. | Come around | d. | Come at |
|---|---|---|---|---|---|---|---|

**A, b, c, d**

197) Our discussion ***continued*** for hours.
198) I have ***submitted*** my claim before the commission.
199) **Visit** us sometime.
200) She **attacked** me with a knife.

# 51 to 100 Sets of Questions

**Set 51:**

| a. | Come at | b. | Run out | c. | Put off | d. | Put on |
|---|---|---|---|---|---|---|---|

**B, c, d, a**

201) The garrison didn't surrender until provisions were ***exhausted***.
202) Getting back home, we ***removed*** our clothes.
203) ***Wear*** your dress, we'll go for a long drive.
204) We're getting nowhere—let's ***think about*** it from another angle.

**Set 52:**

| a. Put out | b. Come by | c. Run over | d. Put on |
|---|---|---|---|

**C, d, a, b**

205) An old man was ***knocked down*** by a lorry.
206) You needn't ***disguise*** a gentleman.
207) The fire brigade team successfully ***extinguished*** the fire.
208) How did you ***get*** his purse?

**Set 53:**

| a. Put out | b. Come down | c. Clear away | d. Run through |
|---|---|---|---|

**D, a, b, c**

209) Bullets ***pierced*** the body of the escaping terrorist.
210) He is a good man. He always ***extends*** his hands to others.
211) Don't ***criticize*** her so hard.
212) The mist has ***dispersed*** after the sunrise.

**Set 54:**

| a. Break away | b. Put out | c. Run through | d. Break down |
|---|---|---|---|

**C, b, a, d**

213) I ***examined*** the book ***quickly*** and bought one for myself.
214) He ***stretched out*** his hand to take the book from the table.
215) The prisoner ***escaped*** from captivity.
216) His health **grew worse** under the pressure of work.

**Set 55:**

| a. Put through | b. Run after | c. Break down | d. Put up |
|---|---|---|---|

**B, a, d, c**

217) Do not ***pursue*** money, but who listens to the words?
218) The task was ***continued*** for twelve months.
219) A notice will be ***posted*** soon regarding this.
220) He **collapsed** in the middle of his speech.

**Set 56:**

| a. Run away | b. Break out | c. Break into | d. Pull apart |
|---|---|---|---|

**A, d, c, b**

221) Leo ***left home*** and joined the army.
222) Failing to yield to me, they criticized me ***unfavorably***.
223) Dacoits ***entered*** the building ***by force*** last night.
224) A devastating fire ***suddenly started*** due to a short circuit.

**Set 57:**

| a. Pull down | b. Run out | c. Break up | d. Run away with |
|---|---|---|---|

**D, c, b, a**

225) The dog ***stole*** a piece of meat.
226) They ***ended*** their relationship and entered another soon.
227) Mother looks very ***exhausted*** after working for the last three hours.
228) The municipal authority decided to ***demolish*** the old buildings in the locality to avoid further loss of lives.

**Set 58:**

| a. Break out from | b. Run over | c. Pull-in | d. Burst in |
|---|---|---|---|

**C, b, a, d**

229) He is ***earning*** a lot of money publishing books of high quality.
230) In the rainy season, the river's water ***overflows*** its banks yearly.
231) Several prisoners ***escaped by breaking out of*** jail.
232) My friend ***suddenly entered*** my house and informed me of my father's accident.

**Set 59:**

| a. Burst on | b. Pull-in | c. Pick at/on | d. Pick out |
|---|---|---|---|

**B, a, d, c**

233) He was ***detained (arrested)*** by SEBI for questioning.
234) We were tense when he ***suddenly appeared on*** the scene.
235) Why do you always ***find fault with*** me?
236) He ***played*** Italian tunes on the piano.

**Set 60:**

| a. Pull-in | b. Burst forth | c. Pick out | d. Cast aside |
|---|---|---|---|

**A, b, c, d**

237) The train ***entered the platform*** on time.
238) A tiger ***suddenly came out*** of the jungle.
239) ***Choose*** the correct word from the options and fill in the blanks.
240) He has ***forsaken*** his family for a foolish reason!

**Set 61:**

| a. Castaway | b. Pick up | c. Burst into | d. Pull out of |
|---|---|---|---|

**D, c, b, a**

241) The train ***left*** the station.
242) The woman ***fell into a cry*** at the news of her husband's death.
243) Where did you ***learn*** your English?
244) He ***threw away*** his old clothes and entered the washroom.

**Set 62:**

| a. Burst open | b. Pick up | c. Pull together | d. Cheer on |
|---|---|---|---|

**C, a, b, d**

245) It will be done in a week if we ***work in harmony***.
246) The door ***suddenly and violently opened*** with a gust of wind, and we could see only lightning.

247) The smugglers were ***arrested*** by the police.
248) The audience ***shouts encouragement*** **for** the players in the stadium.

**Set 63:**

| a. Pick up | b. Pull up | c. Call at | d. Burst out |
|---|---|---|---|

**B, d, a, c**

249) He was ***scolded*** for his misconduct.
250) He ***suddenly began*** weeping like a child.
251) I asked her ***to lift me*** on her way home.
252) We ***met*** him at his house.

**THE SECOND SLOT FROM HERE DOWN** 

**Set 64:**

| a. Hand down | b. Bear down | c. Go abroad | d. Act against |
|---|---|---|---|

**D, c, b, a**

253) We should not **do anything against** others' opinions in general.
254) I have never **visited a foreign country** in my lifetime, and yet I am a refugee
255) He is determined to **defeat** all obstacles.
256) The custom has been **passed on to** the present generation.

**Set 65:**

| a Go along | b. Hand in | c. Act for | d. Bear on |
|---|---|---|---|

**C, d, a, b**

257) He is **working on behalf of** his client.
258) These are the issues that **relate to** the welfare of society.
259) As you **continue accepting**, it will soon become interesting.
260) The minister has **given** his resignation to the Governor.

**Set 66:**

| a. Go ahead | b. Bear out | c. Act on | d. Hand on |
|---|---|---|---|

**D, a, c, b**

261) **Pass** the book to your friend
262) All arrangements are **making progress** to celebrate the occasion.
263) He **worked according to** my advice. So, his failure is my responsibility.
264) The report **confirms** the accusation to be true.

**Set 67:**

| a. Blow away | b. Act upon | c. Call at | d. Hand over |
|---|---|---|---|

**C, b, a, d**

265) The train **stops for a short time** at Didcot & Bangor.

266) They **followed** our instructions.
267) The wind **drove away** all dry leaves.
268) The accused was **delivered** to the police by the villagers.

**Set 68:**

| a. Look in | b. Make after | c. Come across | d. Pull at |
|---|---|---|---|

**D, b, c, a**

269) The workers are **trying to remove** the heavy machine.
270) The Royal Bengal tiger **chasing** the deer was a terrible sight on our last trip to Sundarbans.
271) He spoke for a long time, but his meaning wasn't really **understood**.
272) I shall **visit** his house **briefly** when I pass by.

**Set 69:**

| a. Look into | b. Come about | c. Pass off | d. Clear away/out |
|---|---|---|---|

**D, b, a, c**

273) Ask the servant to ***clean*** the table.
274) Can you tell me how the accident **took place**?
275) Don't worry. I'll **enquire** about the matter soon.
276) The train has gradually **come to a halt**.

**Set 70:**

| a. Lay up | b. Cheer up | c. Cast out | d. Pass by |
|---|---|---|---|

**C, b, a, d**

277) If you come to me, I shall not **reject** you.
278) Oh, come on—**perk up**!
279) I am **confined to bed** with a fever.
280) We **go by** her house every day.

**Set 71:**

| a. Catch at | b. Carry about | c. Let in | d. Lash out at |
|---|---|---|---|

**B, a, d, c**

281) He **takes** a folding chair **with him** wherever he goes.
282) A drowning man **tries to seize** a straw.
283) Maizie **suddenly hit** the boy without any provocation.
284) Allow him to **enter**.

**Set 72:**

| a. Lark about / around | b. Bring back | c. Call over | d. Hold up |
|---|---|---|---|

**B, c, d, a**

285) I shall **return** the book tomorrow.
286) The students are **identified** by their roll numbers.
287) He **delayed** for long hours, and we were about to lose our patience.
288) They **enjoyed time in silly ways over** the last few months and are now complaining about their poor result. (the side-effect of love)

**Set 73:**

| a. Blow up | b. Breakthrough | c. Pull down | d. Go down |
|---|---|---|---|

**A, b, d, c**

289) A storm is **blowing fiercely**.
290) Scientists have **invented** new and important inventions in the fight against cancer.
291) The sun **sets in** the west.
292) He looks much **lowered in spirit**.

**Set 74:**

| a. Pull-off | b. Hang about/around | c. Come away from | d. Break in upon |
|---|---|---|---|

**D, c, b, a**

293) The mob **made their way in force to** the meeting and submitted their petition.
294) The plaster has started to **separate from** the wall.
295) Why do you **move suspiciously** in the examination hall?
296) **Remove** the cover and see what's in.

**Set 75:**

| a. Lay about | b. Bring on | c. Carry away | d. Hang together |
|---|---|---|---|

**B, c, d, a**

297) He has **caused** disgrace to himself.
298) He was **driven** by his enthusiasm.
299) You should all **support one another and work together** to achieve success.
300) She began to **scold** him in anger.

**Set 76:**

| a. Keep off | b. Call back | c. Carry away | d. Knock about |
|---|---|---|---|

**B, c, a, d**

301) She said she'd **telephone** me **in return**.

302) Don't get **extremely excited**. Wait, there are more chances.

303) **Refrain** from bad habits.

304) Employees of the Central Govt. have no fixed place to live, and they **lead unsettled lives** in different places.

**Set 77:**

| a. See About | b. Call in | c. Draw to | d. Laugh at sb |
|---|---|---|---|

**B, c, d, a**

305) The National Library has **ordered the return** of all overdue books.

306) I **felt attracted to** Priya from the first day.

307) The experts **make fun of** my accent, but I don't care; I always ignore them.

308) He says he won't help, does he? Well, we'll soon ***deal with*** that.

**Set 78:**

| a. Carry off | b. Catch out | c. Laugh off / Laugh away | d. Lay down |
|---|---|---|---|

**A, b, c, d**

309) COVID-19 has **taken the lives of** many of our brothers and sisters.

310) Many investors were **surprised** by the fall in share price.

311) I **didn't take** his suggestion about my resignation from the post **seriously**.

312) No such rules are **written** in the book of the Constitution.

**Set 79:**

| a. Turn about | b. Take after | c. Go about | d. Get back to sb |
|---|---|---|---|

**D, c, b, a**

313) I'll find out and **write** a **reply** to you.

314) A strong rumor **spreads** that he will leave us shortly.

315) The child ***resembles*** its mother.

316) The boys ***canceled*** the program and hurried home.

**Set 80:**

| a. Work on | b. Give up | c. Go about | d. Write off |
|---|---|---|---|

**B, c, a, d**

317) **Quit** bad habits if you want to improve your life.

318) I hate **having to move door to door** to promote my book.

319) The workers **continued** working throughout the day and night, and the road was completed in record time.

320) The loss was **canceled in writing**.

**Set 81:**

| a. Set (sb) up | b. Get back | c. Get down | d. Set-off |
|---|---|---|---|

**B, c, d, a**

321) She's **obtained** her old job.
322) Did you **write down** his address?
323) He **began** drawing Lord Shiba.
324) The local people ***produce*** Ramesh, their candidate in the Panchayat election.

**Set 82:**

| a. Work in | b. Turn out | c. Give off | d. Get around |
|---|---|---|---|

**D, c, b, a**

325) Do you find any way of **solving** the problem?
326) The fire **emitted** dense smoke.
327) The man must be **driven out** of here. He is continuously making a nuisance of himself.
328) Please try to ***introduce*** a few more illustrations on the subject.

**Set 83:**

| a. Bear up | b. Act upon | c. Go by | d. Aim at |
|---|---|---|---|

**B, d, a, c**

329) **Based on** the news, I went there.
330) Riya **targets** nothing.
331) The soldiers **sustained** their courage against all odds.
332) They spoke of days **passed**.

**Set 84:**

| a. Bring about | b. Go upon | c. Break off | d. Go up |
|---|---|---|---|

**C, a, d, b**

333) He **stopped speaking** in the middle of his speech.
334) Her ego and folly have **caused** her ruin.
335) The price of essential commodities is **increasing**.
336) He does not **follow** any fixed principles.

**Set 85:**

| a. Go by | b. Blow over | c. Lash out at | d. Carry off |
|---|---|---|---|

**B, d, a, c**

337) The storm will soon **pass**, and the weather will be fine and pleasant.
338) He **won** all the prizes.
339) You cannot always **judge** a book by its cover.
340) In an article, Peter **criticized** all his critics **bitterly**.

**Set 86:**

| a. Go out | b. Bring back | c. Go for | d. Come away with |
|---|---|---|---|

**B, c, a, d**

341) The sight of the village **recalled** old memories.
342) Shall I **fetch** a doctor?
343) **Leave the house to go** in the sun.
344) We **left the place with** the impression that all was not well with their marriages.

**Set 87:**

| a. Hold by | b. Call away | c. Bring forward | d. Hang on |
|---|---|---|---|

**C, b, d, a**

345) All these matters were **presented** in the meeting for discussion.
346) She **stopped and left** the meeting to receive an urgent phone call.
347) I prefer not to **depend on** others for my livelihood.
348) Only true friends **adhere to** you in your difficult times.

**Set 88:**

| a. Grow apart from | b. Set aside | c. Bring on | d. Fall through |
|---|---|---|---|

**C, d, a, b**

349) The damp weather has **led to** his illness.
350) Our holiday plans **flopped** due to heavy rains.
351) The happiest couple **separated** last year.
352) The High Court **put** the judgment of the lower court **on one side**.

**Set 89:**

| a. Burst in | b. Call for (sth) | c. Come around | d. Make up a quarrel |
|---|---|---|---|

**A, b, c, d**

353) We were talking, then a beggar **interrupted** us, seeking help.
354) The matter **demanded** an explanation of his conduct.
355) He'll never **change** our way of thinking.
356) They **developed a misunderstanding**, and that ended with their deaths.

**Set 90:**

| a. Pass off well | b. Keep at | c. Come before | d. Call back |
|---|---|---|---|

**D, c, b, a**

357) I'm waiting for Uday to **telephone** me **in return**.
358) The case **is to be presented before** the court next week.
359) We need to **stick to** our principles.
360) The ceremony **was a success**.

**Set 91:**

| a. Drawback | b. Run down | c. Drop by | d. Send forth |
|---|---|---|---|

**A, c, b, d**

361) The chairman **receded,** declaring the time-table of the innings.
362) Some friends **made short visits** to see me.
363) The man was **run over** by a reckless lorry on the Rajpath.
364) He opened his mouth and **produced a sound to signal** his men.

**Set 92:**

| a. Run through | b. Drop away | c. Fall away | d. Set forth |
|---|---|---|---|

**B, c, a, d**

365) His friends **became fewer** as his fame grew.
366) He has **become lean** since I saw him last.
367) Most of us ***waste our fortune on a chance*** to get a government appointment.
368) Leon ***exhibits*** his views in his books.

**Set 93:**

| a. Get off | b. Send away | c. Fall on/upon | d. Take off |
|---|---|---|---|

**C, a, b, d**

369) The full cost of the ceremony is **incurred by** the students.
370) **Stop touching** me. That hurts!
371) I'm **mailing** the files to my boss tomorrow.
372) ***Remove*** your hands ***from*** my shoulders.

**Set 94:**

| a. Set off/ set | b. Get at sb | c. Come by | d. Pick sth up |
|---|---|---|---|

**C, b, d, a**

373) She **made a short visit** to the house.
374) She always **criticizes** me.
375) Do you **collect** the bags from my aunt when you return?

376) Nicole **started** for Japan.

**Set 95:**

| a. Run-away | b. Cutaway | c. Do in | d. Put down |
|---|---|---|---|

**B, c, d, a**

377) They trimmed the plants, **clipping** the uneven branches.

378) The young actress was so depressed that she felt like **killing** herself.

379) **Write** only the names of the first and second according to the group event.

380) They had an **easy** victory in the match.

**Set 96:**

| a. Cut off | b. Do-over | c. Deal with | d. Put up with |
|---|---|---|---|

**a, c, b, d**

381) The baby is **separated** from its mother.

382) They try to **behave** politely **with** the customers.

383) He was **attacked and injured severely** by a gang of anti-socials.

384) None can **tolerate** such behavior.

**Set 97:**

| a. Cut up | b. Put on | c. Deal in | d. Run across |
|---|---|---|---|

**A, c, b, d**

385) He **cut** the bread **into pieces**.

386) The book **provides** details about Phrase,

387) The blame was **placed upon** me.

388) I **met by chance** my old friend at the ceremony after about a decade.

**Set 98:**

| a. Don (contraction of 'Do on') | b. Doff (contraction of 'do off') | c. Do with | d. Do up |
|---|---|---|---|

**B, a, d, c**

389) **Take off** your coat.

390) **Put on** your coat.

391) We are having the kitchen **repaired**.

392) A politician has to **deal with** all sorts of men.

**Set 99:**

| a. Run up | b. Drop off | c. Fall behind | d. Run at |
|---|---|---|---|

**B, c, d, a**

393) I always **fell asleep** during the long prayer on each Sunday.

394) France **failed to keep pace with** Germany in coal production.

395) The tiger **chases** the deer.

396) The boys **hoisted** a flag on the pole.

**Set 100:**

| a. Set in | b. Sendoff | c. Get along with | d. Get ahead |
|---|---|---|---|

**D, c, b, a**

397) She wants to **make further progress** in her career.

398) It is the right time **to be friendly** with all your enemies and establish peace with them.

399) The data I **discharged** to my H.M. has not reached him.

400) The rainy season has **begun**.

# 101 to 150 Sets of Questions

**Set 101:**

| a. Send on | b. Getaway | c. Get back at sb | d. Set down |
|---|---|---|---|

**B, c, a, d**

401) We hope to **have a holiday** for a few days at Easter.

402) Finally, the rabbit **avenged** the rat and drove it away.

403) We **shipped** our furniture **to** Malaysia.

404) The car ***left*** me to ***descend*** on the way.

**Set 102:**

| a. Set out | b. Get into | c. Get down | d. See off |
|---|---|---|---|

**C, b, d, a**

405) **Have** his consent **in written form** by the evening.

406) Father **admitted** me **to** a High School.

407) The home team ***defeated*** the challengers by 68 runs.

408) He ***disperses*** his goods for display.

**Set 103:**

| a. Get at | b. Send up to | c. Get down | d. Set up |
|---|---|---|---|

**A, c, b, d**

409) The fox could not **reach** the grapes.

410) He **knelt** and sought an excuse for his misconduct.

411) Fifty boys have been **referred** for higher studies **in** Canada.

412) They ***raised*** *a* hue and cry, and a large crowd gathered.

**Set 104:**

| a. Get down | b. Turn on | c. Write off | d. Set up |
|---|---|---|---|

**A, d, b, c**

413) **Move down** the box from the table.
414) He ***began his profession*** as a lawyer.
415) The case ***depends on*** his report.
416) **Prepare quickly** a concise account of your performance over the last year at your previous company.

**Set 105:**

| a. Work out | b. Turn off | c. Turn on | d. Use up |
|---|---|---|---|

**B, c, d, a**

417) ***Switch off*** the light.
418) ***Switch on*** the light.
419) **Use** your nails and pail **completely** to reach your goal.
420) Scientists have **discovered** a medicine that can cure cancer completely.

**Set 106:**

| a. Turn in | b. Work off | c. Turn out | d. Work out |
|---|---|---|---|

**A, c, b, d**

421) I **went to** bed early last night.
422) His story **proved** to be the best in the competition.
423) You must **reduce** the accumulated work.
424) The players are **undergoing** exercise in the field before the match begins.

**Set 107:**

| a. Work on | b. Work at | c. Turn out | d. Turn in |
|---|---|---|---|

**D, c, b, a**

425) We saw a hut and **entered** for shelter.
426) The people **assembled** in large numbers to see the sight.
427) The carpenter is ***engaged in making*** the chair.
428) The engine **runs** by burning diesel.

**Set 108:**

| a. Take-up | b. See out | c. Send out | d. Write (sb) down |
|---|---|---|---|

**B, c, a, d**

429) I've had this coat for years, and I'm sure it will **last till the end of my life.**
430) Have the invitations been **dispatched** yet?

431) He **adopted (accepted)** my case.

432) You can **take** him **to be** a useless fellow.

**Set 109:**

| a. Take away | b. See over | c. Stand by | d. Get down to |
|---|---|---|---|

**D, b, c, a**

433) Let's **begin** our work.

434) We need to ***inspect*** the house before we can extend an offer.

435) In this tumultuous situation, the army is ***ready to support*** the civil authorities.

436) Do not **remove** books from the shelf.

**Set 110:**

| a. Stand over | b. Put through | c. Get behind with | d. Take aback |
|---|---|---|---|

**C, a, d, b**

437) I was **failing to progress** with my work.

438) The question will **be left** for the present.

439) I was **surprised** at the news of his insult in public.

440) After many attempts, the Internet connection was **established**.

**Set 111:**

| a. Get sb down | b. Take by | c. Get up | d. Give over |
|---|---|---|---|

**A, c, d, b**

441) Saying that you only **felt him depressed**.

442) What time does he **wake up**?

443) The accused were **handed over** to the police.

444) The dog **caught** the cat **by** its neck.

**Set 112:**

| a. Take to | b. Give up | c. Give over | d. Work out |
|---|---|---|---|

**C, b, a, d**

445) Before exams, most students **devote themselves to** their studies, which they don't do throughout the year.

446) You should **stop** smoking.

447) I **became fond of** the boy from the beginning.

448) I have **calculated** your share of Rs 10 lac on our farm.

**Set 113:**

| a. Get off with SB | b. Get off to | c. Turn down | d. Turn back |
|---|---|---|---|

**B, a, d, c**

449) I had great difficulty **falling asleep.**
450) Steve **had sex** with Tracey at the party.
451) Don't **send back** a beggar from your door.
452) The principal has **rejected** our proposal.

**Set 114:**

| a. Take into | b. Take in | c. Get on | d. Get off |
|---|---|---|---|

**D, c, b, a**

453) We were lucky to **escape**.
454) I am **making good progress** in my studies.
455) I cannot ***understand*** the meaning of the passage.
456) Before selecting him, his health has to be **considered**.

**Set 115:**

| a. Get into | b. Takedown | c. Take-up | d. Get out |
|---|---|---|---|

**A, d, b, c**

457) Don't **enter** a running train.
458) His secret **became known** to all.
459) ***Register*** the names of the students
460) Mr. Peter **received** the problem to solve.

**Set 116:**

| a. Fall in with | b. Get in /into | c. Take off | d. Take in |
|---|---|---|---|

**A, b, d, c**

461) Finally, he **gave consent to** our decision.
462) What time is the flight expected to **arrive** in Bagdogra from Chennai?
463) He has **enclosed** this plot of land for a garden.
464) The morning bus service will be **withdrawn** from the route from next week.

**Set 117:**

| a. Get about /around | b. Do with | c. Run into | d. Run upon |
|---|---|---|---|

**B, a, c, d**

465) We can no longer **tolerate** his insolvency. (Inability to pay due)
466) She **walks about** with the help of a stick.
467) I **met unexpectedly with** an old friend on the journey.
468) I **was engrossed with** a new idea to publish many booklets on English

Grammar to make them handy.

**Set 118:**

| a. Cut off | b. Cut out | c. Do with | d. Run after |
|---|---|---|---|

**C, b, a, d**

469) He died at an early age.
470) One of the aircraft's engines **stopped functioning.**
471) Please return the book when **finished**.
472) The police **pursued** the thief; they caught and carried him by the neck and shoulder.

**Set 119:**

| a. Put in | b. Come through | c. Deal out | d. Do for |
|---|---|---|---|

**B, c, d, a**

473) A message has **reached** here that you are going to resign.
474) The profits will be **distributed** among the investors.
475) This piece of the stick will **serve** as a scale.
476) I could not **utter** a word among them.

**Set 120:**

| a Put up | b. Tell off | c. Turn out | d. Set about |
|---|---|---|---|

**A, d, b, c**

477) **Raise** a fence around the garden.
478) Paul **started** his packing in the morning.
479) The teacher **scolded** him for quarreling with his classmates.
480) The mill **produces** 100 pairs of clothes every day.

**Set 121:**

| a. Drop in at | b. See-through | c. Drop out | d. See to |
|---|---|---|---|

**A, c, b, d**

481) On my way back, I shall **pay a casual visit** to her house.
482) This is the list of those who ***have stopped attending school*** this year.
483) Her courage and humor led her **to be considered** for the post.
484) Will you **deal with** the arrangements for our next meeting?

**Set 122:**

| a. Put in | b. Get around | c. Give in | d. Run away with |
|---|---|---|---|

**B, c, a, d**

485) He knows well how to **influence** his first customers' views.
486) The powerful soldiers somehow **surrendered**, and the citizens were

saved from the inevitable deaths at their hands.

487) Mr. Dutta has **completed** twenty years of service in teaching.

488) The business proposal will **incur** significant expenses.

**Set 123:**

| a. Pull up | b. Look at | c. Getaway | d. Come on |
|---|---|---|---|

**D, c, b, a**

489) The project is **growing** nicely.

490) The culprit can't **go unpunished**.

491) **See** the birds sitting on the tower.

492) I **stopped**, and I saw a traffic police officer waving his hands.

**Set 124:**

| a. Come down from | b. Come down | c. Pick up | d. Pull through |
|---|---|---|---|

**B, a, c, d**

493) The rain **fell** in torrents.

494) The name **dates back** to the last century.

495) The share price has not **improved in** recent days.

496) He is in great difficulty, but he will **overcome** if we offer him a little help.

**Set 125:**

| a. Pulled out from behind | b. Layout | c. Come down from | d. Let up |
|---|---|---|---|

**C, b, d, a**

497) He has **come down** from Ireland.

498) The garden is well **decorated**.

499) The pain finally **became less intense**.

500) The lorry **overtook** the car.

**Set 126:**

| a. Set down | b. Get sth down | c. Get up | d. Set-off |
|---|---|---|---|

**B, c, a, d**

501) I **swallowed** the medicine **with great difficulty**!

502) The train **arrived** late.

503) The police **recorded** the woman's complaint.

504) The gains were **balanced** against losses.

**Set 127:**

| a. Run against | b. Put aside | c. Get back in | d. Do-over |
|---|---|---|---|

**D, c, b, a**

505) We are **decorating** the drawing room.
506) Will communists ever **return to power** in West Bengal?
507) **Stop** your work **for some time** and listen to me.
508) Peter is **fighting against** odd situations with the shopkeepers.

**Set 128:**

| a. Draw in | b. Deal in | c. Deal with | d. Put through |
|---|---|---|---|

**B, c, a, d**

509) He **trades** rice.
510) He **solved** the difficult problem easily.
511) The Rajdhani Express is **entering the station**.
512) The trainers in the Military Academy **had to undergo** a rigorous schedule.

**Set 129:**

| a. Run along | b. Do with | c. Run over | d. Do without |
|---|---|---|---|

**A, b, d, c**

513) Now, children, **be off**!
514) What will you **make of** these matchsticks?
515) He can hardly **manage anything except** his private secretary.
516) She **glanced over** the pages **hastily** before entering the examination hall.

**Set 130:**

| a. Draw up | b. Run into | c. Run to | d. Fall apart |
|---|---|---|---|

**A, d, b, c**

517) He **wrote out** the contract.
518) Their marriage finally **ended**.
519) The publication has **continued** for ten editions.
520) The money required for the promotion **amounts** to a few lakhs of rupees.

**Set 131:**

| a. Get along | b. Set up | c. Set on/upon | d. Take upon |
|---|---|---|---|

**A, c, b, d**

521) It's time we ***left*** the place.
522) The dogs were ***allowed to attack*** the convict immorally.
523) They ***founded*** a new school.
524) He ***took responsibility for*** the family.

**Set 132:**

| a. Set to/in | b. Set out | c. Get across | d. Give back |
|---|---|---|---|

**C, d, b, a**

525) Your meaning wasn't **realized/understood.**
526) Could you **return** my book?
527) They ***started*** for the picnic spot early in the morning.
528) Let us ***begin*** work at once.

**Set 133:**

| a. Take from | b. Take up with | c. Line up | d. Get at |
|---|---|---|---|

**C, d, a, b**

529) The game teacher asked his students to **get in line**.
530) In this situation, the truth is hard to **find out**.
531) This will **lower** your reputation as a teacher.
532) I was **absorbed in** a book.

**Set 134:**

| a. Get about /around | b. Fall for | c. Run up | d. Take (sb) on |
|---|---|---|---|

**B, a, c, d**

533) Mr. P **yields to the charm of** every beauty only to see hardly any heart in them.
534) The news soon **spread** (as a rumor) that he had resigned.
535) Our long stay at the Daman Diu Hotel **caused us to incur** a hefty bill.
536) I shall ***accept*** you as ***an opponent*** at table tennis, though we are two best friends at other times.

**Set 135:**

| a. Run on | b. Draw on | c. Put up | d. Fall back upon |
|---|---|---|---|

**B, d, c, a**

537) Evening was **approaching**.
538) The army **had recourse to** a new line of defense.
539) I am **staying for some time** with my friend.
540) The engine **works on** CNG.

**Set 136:**

| a. Run down | b. Do up | c. Cry out against | d. Put forward |
|---|---|---|---|

**C, b, d, a**

541) He **protested** such injustice.
542) Who ***is responsible for arranging*** your room every day?
543) One member of the house **introduced** the proposal to be considered.

544) The tiger **caught** the fox **by chase** and punished it with death.

**Set 137:**

| a. Come on | b. Cut down | c. Put off | d. Put on |
|---|---|---|---|

**A, b, c, d**

545) The rainy season is **beginning** in the coastal areas.

546) The physician advised him to **reduce** his consumption of animal protein.

547) The meeting was **postponed**.

548) He has **added** a lot of weight.

**Set 138:**

| a. Put forth | b. Put away | c. Come over | d. Come from |
|---|---|---|---|

**D, c, b, a**

549) Where do you **live**?

550) Why did you **travel** here?

551) . The patient was suffering, and finally, he had to be **put to death** with legal permission.

552) Trees **generate** new leaves in the rainy season.

**Set 139:**

| a. Cut up | b. Do away with | c. Run about | d. Put up |
|---|---|---|---|

**A, b, d, c**

553) The mother was **upset** at the death of her son.

554) 'Why **abolish** the death penalty?' he said.

555) Rahul Dravid was a dependable player who could **give** stiff resistance against rough bowlers in Test matches.

556) The children started to **hurry from one place to another** in great panic.

**Set 140:**

| a. Cut sb out | b. Cry out | c. Do for | d. Put out |
|---|---|---|---|

**B, a, c, d**

557) Peter **shouted** for help; some heard, and none came.

558) Sonny **defeated** Sophia in the competition.

559) The mutual disbelief **ruins** any relationship.

560) Eyes of Pithwiraj Chowhan were **drawn out** in the camp of enemies.

**Set 141:**

| a. Blow in/into | b. Call up | c. Blow out | d. Wash away |
|---|---|---|---|

**A, c, b, d**

561) The door opens, and the schoolboys **arrive noisily at** the classrooms.

562) Don't **extinguish** the fire. We need it later.

563) She could not **remember** the verse and got zero marks in poems.

564) The little dog was **driven** by the current of the river.

**Set 142:**

| a. Bring round | b. Hang on | c. Go in for | d. Go off |
|---|---|---|---|

**A, c, d, b**

565) The patient was **restored** by the care and attention of the staff.

566) The public will **support** the abolition of this custom.

567) The party **passed** well.

568) Through these years, I **stuck to** the project.

**Set 143:**

| a. Knock out | b. Knock off | c. Hold on /Keep at | d. Call for (sb) |
|---|---|---|---|

**D, c, b, a**

569) I will **ask** you **to pick me up from here** at 7 O'clock.

570) We should **stick to** the course through all opposition.

571) The workers usually **stopped work** at five o'clock.

572) I was **overwhelmed** by the news.

**Set 144:**

| a. Keep in | b. Carryout | c. Carry through | d. Lay by/in |
|---|---|---|---|

**B, c, a, d**

573) He agreed to **execute** my orders.

574) He **completed** the work successfully.

575) The fire will **continue (burning)** till tomorrow.

576) **Save** something for the future.

**Set 145:**

| a. Clear off | b. Catch up with | c. Cheer up | d. Clear out |
|---|---|---|---|

**B, c, d, a**

577) Will India **be on the same level as** the developed countries?

578) Bright curtains can **brighten up** a dull room.

579) The sweeper **cleaned** the drain.

580) **Get out** of here.

**Set 146:**

| a. Put out a hand | b. Cut down | c. Do in | d. Cry up |
|---|---|---|---|

**D, b, c, a**

581) A trader **extols** his goods.

582) Please **shorten** your story. It is almost as long as a novel.
583) He looked very **exhausted**.
584) He is a good man. He always **offers help** to others.

**Set 147:**

| a. Lay aside | b. Pull-off | c. Knock up sth | d. Look on |
|---|---|---|---|

**C, a, d, b**

585) Mother **prepared** a meal for us **hurriedly**.
586) We need to **store** something for our bad days.
587) The house **faced** the river.
588) Our team **achieved** a brilliant victory.

**Set 148:**

| a. Go out | b. Holdback | c. Keep out | d. Hang out |
|---|---|---|---|

**A, d, b, c**

589) Don't **run** in the sun.
590) We **spent a long time together** in the boat and passed a pleasant night with a thousand stars over our heads.
591) **Stop** your wrath! It is improper to pass over us like that!
592) I was **put outside of** the business.

**Set 149:**

| a. Clear off | b. Break with | c. Make of | d. Call forth |
|---|---|---|---|

**B, d, a, c**

593) Everyone should **give up** the superstition about religions. There should be only one of Humanity. It means coexistence, cooperation, tolerance, peace, and prosperity for all living beings.
594) Your speech **elicited** an angry response from him.
595) Jack worked overtime to **finish** the arrears of work.
596) What do you **understand** about the words?

**Set 150:**

| a. Call on/upon | b. Keep in | c. Bring round | d. Hang on |
|---|---|---|---|

**C, a, d, b**

597) . After proper counseling, he was **cured**.
598) I now **invite** the chairman to address the meeting.
599) He **kept trying** until we put him down.
600) It is wise to **stay indoors** while it is lightning outside.

# 151 to 184 Sets of Questions

**Set 151:**

| a. Come off | b. Keep off | c. Hang down | d. Call in |
|---|---|---|---|

**D, a, c, b**

601) The National Library has **ordered the return of** all overdue books.
602) When I tried to lift the jug, the handle **separated**.
603) He **bowed** his head with shame, but I was shameless! I kept my head up.
604) Alertness **wards off** many dangers.

**Set 152:**

| a. Keep up | b. Hold on | c. Catch on | d. Call away |
|---|---|---|---|

**D, c, b, a**

605) She ***stopped and left*** the meeting to take an urgent phone call.
606) She is swift to **grasp** things. She is intelligent.
607) The rain **continued** for two hours.
608) Skipper Cook always **maintained** pressure on the Indian team.

**Set 153:**

| a. Lap sth up | b. Keep under | c. Knockdown | d. Carry on |
|---|---|---|---|

**D, b, c, a**

609) I am **continuing** the work while he is away.
610) Please **check and control** your temper.
611) The building was **destroyed**.
612) It's a terrible movie, but audiences everywhere accept it **with great enthusiasm**.

**Set 154:**

| a. Clear out | b. Put forth | c. Come upon | d. Castaway |
|---|---|---|---|

**D, a, c, b**

613) The ship was **wrecked** on the coast of Africa.
614) Please **leave** my room.
615) We **found, by chance,** some boys playing in the field. We sought help from them.
616) I **exerted** all my energy on this task and was able to complete it in seven days.

**Set 155:**

| a. Come along | b. Look for | c. Make for | d. Pass off |
|---|---|---|---|

**A, b, c, d**

617) When the right opportunity **arrives**, she'll take it.
618) I am **searching for** the file that has a yellow cover.
619) I **started for** Delhi, then had to call off, and I got down at Kanpur Station to return.
620) He should be punished for trying to **deceive with** false coins.

**Set 156:**

| a. Come between | b. Point out | c. Pick up | d. Put back |
|---|---|---|---|

**A, c, b, d**

621) I hate anything **that damages the tie between** us.
622) Where were you **affected by** malaria?
623) He **drew the audience's attention** with his views and secured his victory in the coming election.
624) **Restore** the book to its proper place.

**Set 157:**

| a. Bring off | b. Lap up | c. Pass off worse | d. Come across |
|---|---|---|---|

**A, d, b, c**

625) Our football team **won** a grand victory.
626) I hoped she'd **supply** me with some more information.
627) The calf **drank all** the buckets of milk.
628) The ceremony **was unsuccessful**.

**Set 158:**

| a. Come through | b. Bring to | c. Go over | d. Call for (sth) |
|---|---|---|---|

**A, b, d, c**

629) May your father **recover** soon.
630) The girl fainted, but she was soon **revived**.
631) The boss **demanded** an explanation for his conduct.
632) Please **examine** the accounts.

**Set 159:**

| a. Break out *from* | b. Lapse into | c. Go through | d. Mock at |
|---|---|---|---|

**A, c, b, d**

633) Several prisoners **escaped by breaking out of** jail.
634) My father **experienced** great suffering during those twenty minutes, and he died.
635) The patient **gradually passed into** a Coma soon after the accident.
636) She **ignored** me and went away.

**Set 160:**

| a. Look for | b. Bring under | c. Catch up in | d. Hang up |
|---|---|---|---|

**B, c, d, a**

637) Her indomitable spirit can't be **subdued.**

638) Innocent passers-by **accidentally became involved in** the riots.

639) I **cut short** the phone call and put down the receiver.

640) We **expected** better treatment from your son-in-law

**Set 161:**

| a. Go at | b. Let sb/sth down | c. Break forth | d. Call up |
|---|---|---|---|

**C, d, a, b**

641) The sun **suddenly came out** from the clouds, and Arjuna killed Jayadratha.

642) **Make a telephone call to** Rahim to save you from this crisis.

643) They are **making the best possible effort** to complete the road in due time.

644) Edith speaks French very fluently, but her pronunciation **makes** her **less successful**, like Peter in English.

**Set 162:**

| a. Carry through | b. Go back upon/from | c. Look down upon/at | d. Break in /into |
|---|---|---|---|

**D, a, b, c**

645) The robbers **forced their way in** at night and took away all with them.

646) Only courage **helped** him **to overcome** this crisis.

647) I must not **fail to keep** my word.

648) He **derides** them as if they were his eternal slaves, and he is the Lord, equal to God.

**Set 163:**

| a. Call for (sb) | b. Hang upon | c. Cast about for | d. Pass through |
|---|---|---|---|

**A, c, b, d**

649) I will **ask** you **to pick me up from here** at 7 O'clock.

650) He is **looking for** an opportunity to escape.

651) The crowd **listened attentively** to the leader's words.

652) Crude oil **goes through** the pipe.

**Set 164:**

| a. Carryout | b. Come | c. Pass | d. Lay |
|---|---|---|---|

| | across | through | in/by/up |
|---|---|---|---|

**A, b, d, c**

653) I will **fulfill** what I have promised. However, I know I always forget.
654) Father **found** what he had lost **by chance** five months before.
655) Hoarders **stored** food for the future.
656) The crew of the boat **underwent** terrible suffering.

**Set 165:**

| a. Bring back to | b. Clear up | c. Cast off(sth) | d. Come round |
|---|---|---|---|

**A, c, b, d**

657) The change of place **restored** him **to** his health.
658) I am trying to **shun** my poor image so that they think twice.
659) The sky is **becoming clear**.
660) The father was soon **cured of** his illness and began to mix with us.

**Set 166:**

| a. Look forward to | b. Catch up with | c. Let sb off | d. Hold off / keep aloof |
|---|---|---|---|

**B, d, c, a**

661) You guys go on. I'll **reach** you **faster**.
662) Milo should **maintain a distance** from such agitation.
663) I **refuse to let him fall into** the situation. It is my problem. Let me handle this alone.
664) We were **expecting** our uncle's visit **with pleasure** during that time. He brought gifts and blessings for us all.

**Set 167:**

| a. Break-in | b. Go by | c. Break up | d. Come forward |
|---|---|---|---|

**A, c, d, b**

665) He **interrupted** our serious discussion and asked for a glass of water.
666) Our school will **close** from next Saturday.
667) He **moved ahead** and offered his help.
668) I shall **follow** my teachers' advice.

**Set 168:**

| a. Call to | b. lay by/up | c. keep off | d. Grow back |
|---|---|---|---|

**A, d, c, b**

669) I **addressed** my friend **loudly** from the roof.
670) The plant **returned to its previous length** after it was trimmed.

671) **Avoid** bad company.
672) He **stored** enough for the future.

**Set 169:**

| a. Cast down | b. Look to | c. Pull out of | d. Come after |
|---|---|---|---|

**A, d, b, c**

673) He is easily **depressed**. However, you can't say he tends to commit suicide.
674) The night guard **chased** the thief; however, the thief managed to escape.
675) I **rely on** you for help.
676) He had **come out of** difficult situations

**Set 170:**

| a. Break-in | b. Come over | c. Go down | d. Catch up on |
|---|---|---|---|

**A, d, b, c**

677) The horses are being **trained**.
678) I have a lot of things to **spend extra time on**.
679) He will never **change sides** to our side.
680) P. Bose **descends from** the clan of Netaji.

**Set 171:**

| a. Go over | b. Go down with | c. Break off | d. Bring back |
|---|---|---|---|

**C, d, b, a**

681) Sophia **separated** her engagement with Felix.
682) The sight of the village **recalled** old memories.
683) He has **suffered from** fever.
684) He **changed sides** to the opposition party.

**Set 172:**

| a. Breakthrough | b. Go through | c. Let sb out of | d. Hold out |
|---|---|---|---|

**A, b, d, c**

685) Luis Suarez **found a way against** the defense of his rival team.
686) I heard the proposal **was accepted** without any opposition.
687) The doctor **had** little hope of his recovery.
688) Counselling is important to **help her come out of** depression.

**Set 173:**

| a. Makeover | b. Break up into | c. Go for | d. Lookup |
|---|---|---|---|

**B, c, d, a**

689) The ship was **torn into** parts in the clash against the rock underwater.

690) He **receives** a scholarship here since he was a gold medalist in his graduation.

691) Please **visit** us on your return from London.

692) The principal **handed over the** charge to me.

**Set 174:**

| a. Go out | b. Pullover | c. Go on | d. Call at… (of a train) |
|---|---|---|---|

**B, d, c, a**

693) The driver **stopped** the bus **safely** at the last second and saved us all.

694) The train **stops for a short time** at Didcot & Reading.

695) The meeting **continued** for ten minutes, and we left the place.

696) The lamp has **extinguished** after twelve minutes.

**Set 175:**

| a. Put about | b. Let up | c. Bring down | d. Call forth |
|---|---|---|---|

**C, d, a, b**

697) The price of essential commodities has been **reduced** since last week.

698) Your speech **elicited** an angry response from him.

699) I hear many stories that are **spreading (rumors)**.

700) We mustn't **make less effort** now.

**Set 176:**

| a. Come around | b. Go in for | c. Pull through | d. Come across |
|---|---|---|---|

**D, a, b, c**

701) Kinsley **met** his ex-girlfriend **by chance**. He stepped forward and kissed her forehead, surprising everyone.

702) Your mother has not yet **become conscious** of the anesthetic.

703) We shall **sit for** the next B. Sc's exam.

704) He was critically ill but has **recovered**.

**Set 177:**

| a. Carry (sb) back | b. Come off | c. Go off | d. Come on |
|---|---|---|---|

**A, b, d, c**

705) The incident **transported** him **back** to his past, to his childhood days.

706) When will the festival **take place**?

707) **Hurry**, we will be late for the function.

708) The pistol **was shot** suddenly.

**Set 178:**

| a. Put by | b. Bring down | c. Come down from | d. Come down |
|---|---|---|---|

**B, d, c, a**

709) The enemy aircraft was **forced down by fire**.

710) The new bridge **collapsed** after its inauguration in Kolkata. Minister says, "We look into the matters."

711) She **left** Oxford.

712) Ants **preserve** some food for the winter. Why shouldn't we for our uncertain future?

**Set 179:**

| a. Come down with | b. Brings in | c. Come apart | d. Put across |
|---|---|---|---|

**B, c, a, d**

713) They tried to **introduce** a new fashion in the publication.

714) The glass just **broke into pieces** in my hands.

715) I think I'm **getting affected** by the flu.

716) Jacob failed to **communicate** his views **successfully** to the commission.

**Set 180:**

| a. Go without | b. Come back | c. Come along with | d. Put forward |
|---|---|---|---|

**C, b, a, d**

717) **Accompany** us as we visit a museum.

718) You **returned** very late last night.

719) He has **passed without** food for five days.

720) Dr. R.D. **advanced** a new theory on solar energy that may bring a revolution.

**Set 181:**

| a. Come back in | b. Grow away from (sb) | c. Put in words for (sb) | d. Pull up (with) |
|---|---|---|---|

**A, b, d, c**

721) Long hair for men seems to be **becoming popular again**.

722). They have **become less close**; now, they live in different places.

723) Initially, he was trailing, but soon, he **improved relativity** with others.

724) Please **plead on** my behalf.

**Set 182:**

| a. See out | b. set forth | c. Get back in | d. Get up |
|---|---|---|---|

**B, d, c, a**

725) Sophia **began** her journey around the world last November.
726) The old lady slowly **stood up**, went through the gate, and disappeared.
727) She said she would **speak again to** me **within** a few days.
728) The car has enough fuel to **reach** our destination.

**Set 183:**

| a. set in | b. Pass off | c. Keep in touch | d. Go for |
|---|---|---|---|

**D, c, b, a**

729) Shall I **fetch** a doctor?
730) Are they able to **agree with** us anymore after the incident?
731) The present disturbances will soon **be over**.
732) The summer vacation has ***begun*** in the institution.

**Set 184:**

| a. Hang back | b. Look about for | c. set to | d. Lay on |
|---|---|---|---|

**C, b, d, a**

733) Let us ***start*** work at once.
734) Charlotte is **searching for** a house in the new town.
735) The mother **put** her hand ***on*** her son's head.
736) I am not here to **go back** to my place.

# The List of Phrasal Verbs, Arranged Alphabetically

As mentioned earlier, phrasal verbs are formed of ***verbs with adverbs, prepositions, or both***. To gain a better understanding, it's recommended to study thc following phrasal verbs, which are similar to those used in the above sets, from 1 to 184. A total of 736 phrasal verbs are included in this list, arranged alphabetically. The list begins with the letter 'A'.

## A for 'Act,' 'Aim at,' etc.

| Group Verbs | Examples | Meanings |
|---|---|---|
| Act against | We should not act against others' opinions in general. | Do anything against |
| Act for | He is acting for his client. | Working on behalf of |

| | | |
|---|---|---|
| **Act on** | He acted on my advice. So, his failure is my responsibility. | Worked according to |
| Act upon (1) | The medicine acts upon the heart. | affects |
| Act upon (2) | They acted upon our instructions. | Did as per |
| Act upon (3) | Acting upon the news, I went there. | Based upon/ depending on |
| | | |
| **Aim at** | Riya aims at nothing. | (Wish target or goal/determines to do) |

## B *for* 'Bear,' 'Blow,' 'Break,' 'Bring,' 'Burst'

| Group Verbs | Examples | Meanings |
|---|---|---|
| Back up | He **backed up** his friend's claim. | Supported |
| Bear away | Preston bore away the prize for his talent. | Won |
| Bear down on | He is determined to bear down on all obstacles. | To defeat/ overcome |
| Bear on | These are the issues that bear on the welfare of society. | Relate to/impact |
| Bear out | The report bears out the accusation as true.<br>Dr. Roy will bear out what I'll say. | Support/ confirm |
| Bear up | The soldiers bore up their courage against all odds. | Kept up/ sustained |
| Bear with | I have to bear with her patiently during this challenging period. | tolerate |
| | **Blow** | |
| Blow away | The wind blew away all the dry leaves. | Drove away |
| Blow in/into | The door opened, and the schoolboys blew into the classrooms. | Arrive noisily, cheerfully. |
| Blow off | The chimneys blow off thick smoke. | Emit |
| Blow out | Don't blow out the fire. We need it later. | Extinguish /put out. |
| Blow over | • The storm will soon blow over, and the weather will be fine and pleasant.<br>• The present disturbances will soon **blow over**. | (Pass off)/ disappear |

| | | |
|---|---|---|
| Blow up (1) | Opponent soldiers **blew up** the buildings. | (exploded) |
| Blow up (2) | A storm is blowing up. | Blowing fiercely |
| Blow up (3) | You don't need to blow up your credits. | Exaggerate |
| | **Break** | |
| Break away | The prisoner broke away from captivity.<br>The accused broke away from the lock-up | Escaped suddenly/ freed himself |
| Break away from | Everyone should *break away from* superstition about religion. There should be only one religion of humanity, which means coexistence, cooperation, tolerance, peace, and prosperity for all living beings. | Give up/stop following |
| Break down (1) | His health broke down under the pressure of work. | Grew worse |
| Break down (2) | He **broke down** in the middle of his speech. | (Failed) collapsed |
| Break forth | The sun broke forth from the clouds, and Arjuna killed Jayadratha. | Suddenly, came out/ appeared. |
| Break in (1) | The robbers broke in at night and took away all with them. | Forced their way in |
| Break in (2) | The horses are being broken in. | Trained |
| Break into (1) | He *broke into* our serious discussion and asked for a glass of water.<br>He broke into the meeting without prior permission and didn't say, 'Sorry'. | Interrupted |
| Break into (2) | Dacoits broke into the building last night. | Entered by force |
| Break into (3) | The ship was broken into parts in the clash against the underwater rock. | Separate or ruin. |
| Break in upon | The mob broke in upon the meeting and submitted their petition. | Made their way in by force (for) |
| Break off (1) | He broke off in the middle of his speech. | Stopped speaking |
| Break off (2) | Sophia broke off her engagement | Ended/separated |

| | | |
|---|---|---|
| | with Felix. | |
| Break out (1) | A devastating fire broke out due to a short circuit. | Started suddenly |
| Break out *of* (2) | Several prisoners broke out of jail. | Escaped by breaking. |
| Breakthrough (1) | Scientists have broken through new and important inventions in the fight against cancer. | Invented or made something new. |
| Breakthrough (2) | Luis Suarez broke through the defense of his rival team. | Found a way against/ forced a passage in |
| Break up (1) | Our school will break up from next Saturday.<br>The meeting broke up at 5 p.m. | Close/end |
| Break up (2) | They **broke up** their relationship and entered another one soon. | Ended relationship |
| | **Bring** | |
| Bring about | • The blind ego, falsity, pretention, and blind love for fantasy will bring about our ruin before time.<br>• Her folly has brought about (caused) her ruin. | Cause |
| Bring back (1) | I shall bring back the book tomorrow. | Return |
| Bring back (2) | The sight of the village brought back old memories. | Reawaken/recall |
| Bring back to | The change of place brought him back to his health. | Restored to |
| Bring down | The prices of essential commodities have been brought down since last week. | Reduced/decreased slightly |
| Bring down | The enemy aircraft was brought down. | Force STH down by firing |
| Bring forth/in | All trees bring forth new, tender leaves during the rainy season. | Produce /beget |
| Bring forward | All these matters were brought forward for discussion in the meeting. | Raised or presented |
| Bring in | My business brings in a good income. | Yields/profits |
| Brings in (2) | They tried to bring new fashion to the publication. | introduce |
| Bring off | Our football team brought off a | won |

| | | |
|---|---|---|
| | grand victory. | |
| Bring on (1) | The damp weather has brought on his illness. | Led to. |
| Bring on (2) | He has brought disgrace to himself. | caused |
| Bring out | My first book was brought out in 2013. It was a book of poems. | published |
| Bring out (2) | Proper training will bring out the best in him. | Reveal, nurture |
| Bring around (1) | Careful nursing brought the patient around. | Made restored to |
| Bring around (2) | After proper counseling, he was brought around. | Made cured /overcome |
| Bring to | The girl fainted, but she was soon brought to her senses. | Revive; to bring (sb) to senses. |
| Bring under | Her indomitable spirit can't be brought under. | subdued |
| Bring up | After the death of his father, he was brought up by his mother. | reared |
| | **Burst** | |
| Burst in | My friend burst into my house and informed me of my father's accident. | *Suddenly entered* |
| Burst in front of | We were talking when a beggar burst in front of us, seeking help. | interrupted |
| Burst onto | We were tense when he burst onto the scene. | Appeared suddenly |
| Burst forth | A tiger burst forth from the jungle | Came out suddenly |
| Burst into | The woman burst into tears at the news of her husband's death. | Fell in cry terribly |
| Burst open | The door burst open with a gust of wind, and we could see only the lightning around. | Open suddenly and violently. |
| Burst out | He burst out weeping like a child. | Suddenly began |

## C *for* 'Call,' 'Carry,' 'Cast,' etc.

### C *for* 'Call', 'Carry', 'Cast', 'Catch', 'Cheered', 'Clear', 'Cling', 'Come', 'Cry', 'Cut'

| Group Verbs | Examples | Meanings |
|---|---|---|
| Call at… (of a train) | The train calls at Didcot & Reading. | To stop at a place for a short time |
| Call at (2) | We called him at his house. | met |

| | | |
|---|---|---|
| Call away | She was called away from the meeting to receive an urgent phone call. | Stopped and gone away; *(ask SB to stop what they are doing to attend to another.)* |
| Call back | • She said she'd call me back.<br>• I'm waiting for Uday to call me back.<br>• Call her back; she said it was urgent.<br>• Do you call me back? | To telephone someone in return; to telephone someone who telephoned you earlier. |
| Call for (sth) | The matter called for an explanation of his conduct. | demanded |
| **Call for (sb)** | I'll call you at 7 O'clock. | Ask SB to receive it from somewhere. |
| Call forth | Your speech called forth an angry response from him. | Elicited /produced a particular reaction |
| Call in (1) | He called in a doctor. | Sent for/ called for help or service |
| Call in (2) | The National Library has called in all overdue books. | Ordered for return |
| Call off | The boss called off the meeting with us to attend to the other. | (canceled) |
| Call on/upon | I now call upon the chairman to address the meeting.<br>I feel called upon to warn you about gambling. | Invite or ask SB to speak/ feel that I ought |
| Call out | The fire brigade was called out by the authorities before it was too late. | Summoned /to ask SB to come in emergency |
| **Call over** | The students are called over by their roll numbers. | Attend/To give attendance. |
| **Call to** | I called my friend from the roof. | Addressed loudly |
| **Call up (1)** | Call up Rahim to save you from this crisis. | To make a telephone call to sb |
| Call up (2) | She could not call up the verse and received zero marks. | Remember /recall STH. |
| Call upon | He was called upon to explain his conduct. | Ordered to be present |
| | **Carry** | |
| Carry away (1) | • His enthusiasm carried him away.<br>• The current of the river carried the little dog away. | driven |

| | | |
|---|---|---|
| Carry away (2) | Don't get carried away. Wait, there are more chances. | Extremely excited |
| Carry back | The incident carried him back to his childhood days. | Returned to the past |
| Carry off | COVID-19 has carried off many of our brothers and sisters. | Took the lives of |
| Carry off (2) | • He carried off all the prizes.<br>• Nicky carried off the best prize. | won |
| Carry on | I am carrying on the work while he is away. | continuing |
| Carry out (1) | I shall carry out what I have promised. However, I know I always forget. | fulfill |
| Carry out (2) | He agreed to carry out_my orders. | (execute) |
| Carry through | Only courage carried him through this crisis. | Helped him to overcome … |
| Carry through | He carried through the work successfully. | completed |
| | **Cast** | |
| Cast about for | He is casting about for an opportunity to escape. | Looking for |
| Cast aside | He has cast aside his family for a foolish reason! | forsaken |
| Castaway (1) | He cast away his old clothes and entered the washroom. | Thrown away. |
| Castaway (2) | The ship was cast away on the coast of Africa. | wrecked |
| Cast down | He is easily cast down. However, you can't say he tends to commit suicide. | depressed |
| Cast off (sth) | I am trying to cast off my poor image so that they think twice. | Shun/ abandon |
| Cast out | If you come to me, I shall not cast you out. | reject |
| | **Catch** | |
| Catch on | She is very quick to catch on to things. She is intelligent. | To grasp or understand sth |
| Catch off guard | Many investors were caught off guard by the decline in share prices. | Surprised and found in a difficult situation |
| Catch up on | I have many things to catch up on. | To spend extra time (doing new things). |

| | | |
|---|---|---|
| Catch up in | Innocent passers-by got caught up in the riots. | To become involved accidentally |
| Catch up with (1) | • Go on ahead; I'll catch up with you.<br>• Don't wait for me. You guys go on. I will go on my bike & catch up with you soon. | To reach SB, who is ahead, by going faster than him. |
| Catch up with (2) | Will India catch up with the developed countries? | To be at the same level (improving faster than others) |
| | **Cheer** | |
| Cheer on | The audience cheered the players on in the stadium. | To give shouts of encouragement in sports |
| Cheer up | • Oh, come on—cheer up!<br>• Give Mary a call; she needs cheering up.<br>• Bright curtains can cheer up a dull room. | Perk up /enliven/ brighten up (To make sb or sth cheerful) |
| | **Clear** | |
| Clear away/out | Ask the servant to ***clear away*** the table.<br>The sweeper ***cleared out*** the drain. | To clean |
| Clear away (2) | The mist has cleared away after the sunrise. | dispersed |
| Clear off | Jack worked overtime to clear off the arrears of work. | To finish or complete |
| Clear off (2) | Clear off from here. | Get out |
| Clear out (2) | Please clear out my room. | Leave |
| Clear up | The sky is clearing up. | Gets rid of clouds/ becomes clear |
| Cling to | A drowning man clings to a straw. | clutches |
| | **Come** | |
| Come about | When did the accident come about?<br>Can you tell me how it came about? | Happen/ take place. |
| Come across (1) | He spoke for a long time, but his meaning didn't come across. | Appear to sense/understand |
| Come across (2) | Kinsley came across his ex-girlfriend. He stepped forward and kissed her forehead, surprising everyone. | Met by chance |

| | | |
|---|---|---|
| Come across (3) | The father came across the thing he had lost five months before. | Found a thing by chance |
| Come across (4) | I hoped she'd come across with some more information. | To provide or supply what you need |
| Come after | The night guard came after the thief; however, the thief escaped. | chased |
| Come along (1) | Come along; it is getting late. | hurry |
| Come along (2) | When the right opportunity comes along, she'll take it. | To arrive /appear |
| Come apart | The book just came apart in my hands. | To break into pieces |
| Come around | Your mother has not yet come around from the anesthetic. | Come to your senses again. |
| Come around (2) | Do come around and see us sometime. | To visit a place for a short time |
| Come around (3) | He'll never come around to our way of thinking. | Change one's mood or opinion. |
| Come at (1) | She came at me with a knife. The rioters came at us last night with swords and other weapons. | attacked |
| Come at (2) | We're getting nowhere—let's come at it from another angle. | To think about a problem or situation from a different angle |
| Come away from | The plaster has started to come away from the wall. | separate from |
| Come away with | We came away with the impression that all was not well with their marriage. | To leave a place with a particular feeling or impression |
| Come back | You came back very late last night. | Returned |
| Come back in | Long hair for men is coming back in. | To become popular again |
| Come before | The case is scheduled to come before the court next week. | to be presented |
| Come between | I hate anything that comes between us. | That damage (a tie or relationship between) |
| Come by (1) | She came by the house. | Made a short visit |
| Come by (2) | How did you come by his purse? | (Get)/Obtain |

| | | |
|---|---|---|
| Hard to come by | Jobs are ***hard to come by*** these days. | scarce |
| Come down (1) | The new bridge came down after its inauguration in Kolkata. Minister says, "We look into the matters." | collapsed |
| Come down (2) | The rain came down in torrents. | fell |
| Come down from (1) | She came down from Oxford. | To leave a university |
| Come down from (2) | He has come down from North Bengal.<br>He has come down from China. | From one place to another, generally from north to south. |
| Come down from (3) | The name has come down from the last century. | Dates back to |
| Come down on | Don't come down so hard on her. | Censure SB/ punish |
| Come down with | I think I'm coming down with the flu. | Getting affected/or getting an illness |
| Come forward | He came forward and offered his help. | Move ahead (Voluntarily give help or information) |
| Come from | Where do you come from? | The place where someone lives |
| Come of | B. R. Ambedkar came from a poor family. | Was born in |
| Come off (1) | When will the festival come off? | Take place |
| Come off (2) | When I tried to lift the jug, the handle came off. | Became separated from |
| Come on (1) | The project is coming on nicely. | Growing |
| Come on (2) | Come on, we will be late for the function. | Hurry |
| Come on (3) | The rainy season is coming on in the coastal areas. | Beginning |
| Come out (1) | The rain stopped, and the sun came out. | appeared |
| Come out (2) | When is your next book coming out? | Publishing |
| Come over (1) | He will never come over to our side. | Change side |
| Come over (2) | Why did you come over here? | travel |

| | | |
|---|---|---|
| Come around | Father came around his illness soon and began to mix with us. | (recovered from /cured of) |
| Come through (1) | A message has come through here that you are going to resign. | Received/reached |
| Come through (2) | May your father come through soon. | Recover/ come round. |
| Come upon | We came upon some boys playing in the field. We sought help from them. | Found by chance |
| | **Cry** | |
| Cry down | Don't cry down his achievements. Think of what labor he gave, we couldn't. | Underestimate /decry |
| Cry off | We said we would go but had to cry off at the last moment. | Abandon/cancel. |
| Cry to | The helpless man cried to the rioters for his life. | begged |
| Cry up | A trader cries up his goods. | Extols/ exaggerates |
| Cry out | Peter cried out for help, but no one heard, and no one came. | Shouted loudly |
| Cry out against | He cried out against such injustice. | Protest sth |
| | **Cut** | |
| Cutaway | They trimmed the plants, cutting away the uneven branches. | clipping |
| Cut down (1) | Please cut down your story. It is almost as long as a novel. | Shorten |
| Cut down (2) | The physician advised him to cut down his consumption of animal protein. | reduce |
| Cut in on | She kept ***cutting in on*** our conversation. | Interrupting |
| Cut off (1) | The baby is cut off from its mother. | Separated |
| Cut off (2) | He was cut off at an early age. | Died |
| Cut out (1) | One of the aircraft's engines cut out. | Stopped functioning |
| Cut out (2) | Maizie was cut out for this job. | Suitable |
| Cut out (3) | Sonny cut Sophia out of the competition. | defeated |
| Cut up (1) | The mother was cut up at the death of her son. | Upset |
| Cut up (2) | He cut up the bread. | Cut (sth) into pieces |

## D *for* 'Deal,' 'Do,' 'Draw,' etc.

| *Group Verbs* | *Examples* | *Meanings* |
|---|---|---|
| Deal in (1) | He deals in rice. | Trades |
| Deal in (2) | The book deals in detail with Phrases, Clauses & sentences. | provides |
| Deal out | The profits will be dealt out among the investors. | distributed |
| Deal with (1) | They try to deal politely with the customers. | Behave with |
| Deal with (2) | He dealt with the difficult problem easily. | Solved. |
| Deal with (3) | A politician has to deal with all sorts of men. | Do with |
| Deal with (4) | Peter is dealing with unusual situations involving the shopkeepers. | Cope or adjust with |
| | **Do** | |
| Do away with (1) | 'Why do away with the death penalty?' he said. | abolish |
| Do away with (2) | The woman attempted to ***do away with*** herself. | Take her own life |
| Do for (1) | Mutual disbelief **does for** any relationship. | ruins |
| Do for (2) | This piece of stick will do for a scale. | Serve as / to be used as |
| **Doff** (contraction of 'do off') | Doff your coat. | Take off |
| **Don** (contraction of 'Do on') | Don your coat. | Put on |
| Do something to (1) | The young actress was so depressed that she felt like doing something to herself. | killing |
| Do in (2) | He looked very done in. | exhausted |
| Do over (1) | He was done over by a gang of anti-socials. | Attacked and injured severely. |
| Do over (2) | We are doing over the drawing room. | decorating |
| Do up (1) | Who is to do up your room every day? | arrange |
| Do up (2) | We are having the kitchen done up. | Repaired. |
| Do with (1) | We can no longer do with his insolvency. (Inability to pay due) | tolerate |
| Do with (2) | What will you do with these | make of; use |

| | | |
|---|---|---|
| | matchsticks? | |
| Do with (4) | Please return the book when you are done with it. | Finished |
| Do without | He can hardly do without his private secretary. | Manage without |
| | **Draw** | |
| Draw away | His attention was drawn away by the loud noise. | Diverted. |
| Drawback | The chairman drew back and declared the timetable of the innings. | Receded/retreated |
| **Draw in** | The Rajdhani Express is drawing in. | Entering the station |
| Draw on | The evening was drawing on. | Approaching |
| Draw out (1) | The girl is very shy and needs to be drawn out to talk. | Encouraged |
| Draw out (2) | The professor drew out the interview with MR. Rahaman intentionally tested his patience for the job. | prolonged |
| Draw to | I was drawn to Priya from the first day. | Felt attracted to |
| Draw up | He drew up the contract. | Wrote out; wrote in full |
| | **Drop** | |
| Drop away | His fame grew, and his friends dropped away. | Became fewer/drop off |
| Drop by | Some friends dropped by to see me. | Made short visits |
| Drop by | On his long journey, he **dropped by** every metropolitan area. | (Stopped for a visit) |
| Drop in at | On my way back, I shall drop in at her house. | Pay a casual visit. |
| Drop off | My friends dropped off one by one after we got married, and everyone. | Reduce in number/become fewer. |
| Drop off (2) | I always dropped off during the long prayer on each Sunday. | Fell asleep |
| Drop out | This is the list of those who have dropped out of school this year, sir. | Leave/ stop to continue. |

## F for 'Fall,' etc.

| Group Verbs | Examples | Meanings |
|---|---|---|
| Fall apart (1) | The glass **fell apart**. | Broke into pieces |
| Fall apart | Their marriage finally fell apart. | ended a |

| | | |
|---|---|---|
| (1) | | relationship |
| Fall away with (1) | The film star's fans ***fell away with*** the decline of his popularity.<br>The film star's fans ***dwindled*** as his popularity waned. | Dwindled /deserted /left him |
| Fall away (2) | The black spots are yet to fall away from your face. | Disappear |
| Fall away much (3) | He has ***fallen away much*** since I saw him last. | Become lean |
| Fall back | The enemy fell back with the advance of our troops. | Retreated |
| Fall back upon | The army fell back upon a new line of defense. | Had recourse to |
| Fall behind | France fell behind Germany in coal production. | Failed to keep level with |
| Fall for | Mr. P falls for every pretty face, only to see hardly any heart in them. | Yields to the charm of |
| Fall in (1) | The game teacher asked his students to fall in. | Get into a line. |
| Fall in (2) | The new building fell in within a year. | Collapsed |
| Fall in with (1) | After a decade, Subba ***fell in with*** his best friend Kanak at the fest. | Met by chance |
| Fall in with (2) | Finally, he fell in with our decision. | Agree/give consent |
| .Fall off (1) | Attendance in classes has fallen off after the exams in schools. | Decreased |
| Fall off (2) | False friends fall off in misfortune. | Drop off |
| Fall on/upon (1) | Miscreants fell on/upon them. | Attacked fiercely |
| Fall on/upon (2) | The full cost of the ceremony fell on the students. | Incurred upon |
| Fall out | The boys fell out with each other over the issue of goals. | Quarreled |
| Fall through | Our holiday plans fell through due to heavy rains. | Failed/ flopped |
| Fall to | He fell to eating with greater gusto. | began |

## G *for* 'Get,' 'Give,' 'Go,' etc.

| *Group Verbs* | *Examples* | *Meanings* |
|---|---|---|
| Get around | • The scandal of his affair with a widow ***got around*** in a day.<br>• News soon ***got around*** that he | Spread (as a rumor) |

| | | |
|---|---|---|
| | had resigned. | |
| Get around | She gets around with the help of a stick. | Move or walk about. |
| Get across | Your meaning didn't get across. | Be realized /understood |
| Get ahead | • She wants to get ahead in her career.<br>• Who doesn't want to get ahead?<br>• She wanted so, and she got ahead. | To make further progress |
| Get along with (1) | It is the right time to **get along with** your enemies and establish peace with them. | (To be friendly with someone) |
| Get along (2) | It's time we got along. | Left the place |
| Get at sb (1) | She always gets at me. | Criticize / attack |
| Get at sth (2) | • The fox could not get at the grapes.<br>• The files are locked up and I can't get at them. | Reach |
| Get at sth (2) | • In this situation, the truth is hard to get at.<br>• The truth is sometimes difficult to get at. | Find out |
| Get away (1) | We're hoping to get away for a few days at Easter. | To have a holiday or vacation |
| Get away (2) | • The prisoner got away last night.<br>• Thieves got away with computer equipment worth three lakhs. | Escaped |
| Get away (3) | • The culprit can't get away.<br>• He can't get away with imprisonment for only three months!<br>• Nobody can get away with insulting me like that. | Go unpunished /receive relatively light punishment. |
| Get back (1) | • When did you get back last night?<br>• When will you get back from there? | Return |
| Get back | • She's got back her old job. | To obtain STH |

| | | |
|---|---|---|
| (2) | • She got back her lost iPhone after six months from the riverbed. | again after having lost it |
| Get back to sb | • Finally, the rabbit **got back at** the rat and drove it away.<br>• I'll find a way of getting back at him! | (To get revenge on somebody) |
| Get back in | • Jadavas finally got back in power in Bihar.<br>• Will communists ever return to West Bengal? | Return to (power or position) |
| Get back to sb | • I'll find out and get back to you.<br>• She said she would get back to me within a few days. | To speak or write again as a reply |
| Get behind with | • I'm getting behind with my work.<br>• He got behind in his profession. | Failing to make enough progress |
| Get by | Most of the salaried men here got by on a small salary. | Managed to live. |
| Get down (1) | Did you get down his address? | Write down |
| Get down (2) | Get his consent down by this evening. | Having something in written form |
| Get down (3) | He got down and sought an excuse for his misconduct. | Knelt down |
| Get SB down | Saying that you only got him down. | Felt him depressed |
| Get STH down | I got the medicine down! | Swallow STH usually with great difficulty |
| Get down to (2) | Let's get down to our work. | Begin |
| Get sth from | Get the box from the table. | Move something |
| Get in /into | • What time is the flight expected to get into Bagdogra from Chennai?<br>• The train got in late. | Arrive |
| Get into (1) | • Father got me into a High School. | Admitted |
| Get into (2) | • He got into trouble with the police while still a student.<br>• I got into a conversation with an | To become involved in/ to reach a condition |

| | | |
|---|---|---|
| | Italian student. | |
| **Get to** | The car has enough fuel to **get to** our destination. | to reach |
| Get off (1) | Get off me, that hurts! | Tell SB to stop touching. |
| Get off/ get sb off | • We got off straight after breakfast.<br>• She got her child off to his school every day.<br>• We got off in the middle of the meeting. | To leave/leave someone at |
| Get off to | I had great difficulty getting off to sleep. | To fall asleep |
| Get off with SB | • Steve got off with Tracey at the party.<br>• Do the youths go there to go off with somebody? | To have sexual or romantic relations with SB |
| Get off (2) | We were lucky to get off. | Escape |
| Get on | I am getting on with my studies. | Making good progress. |
| Get onto | Don't get onto a running train. | Enter |
| Get out (1) | His secret got out to all | Became known |
| Get out | The news of our President's death ***got out*** sooner than we hoped. | spread |
| Get out (2) | Few passengers were lucky to *get out* of the burning train. | escape |
| *Get out of* | Get out of the class. | leave |
| Get over | The old man could not get over the shock of his son's death. | Overcome |
| Get around (1) | He knows well how to get around his first customers with his views. | Influence |
| Get around (2) | Do you find any way of getting around the problem? | Solving |
| Get through (1) | Many students failed the test, and only a few got through. | Passed |
| Get through | Please join us as soon as you get through your task. | Complete |

| | | |
|---|---|---|
| (2) | | |
| Get up (1) | What time does he get up? | Wake up |
| Get up (2) | The old lady slowly got up, went through the gate, and disappeared. | Stood up |
| | **Give** | |
| Give away (1) | The chief guest and others gave away the prizes on the school sports day. | Distributed |
| Give away (2) | The soldier didn't give away any secrets to our enemy. | Reveal |
| Give back | Could you give me back my book? | return |
| Give forth | The engine gave forth much smoke. | emitted |
| Give in | The powerful soldiers somehow **gave in**, and the citizens were saved from the inevitable deaths at their hands. | Surrendered |
| Give off | The fire **gave off** dense smoke. | emitted/gave out |
| Give out (1) | After a few days, our stock of rice will give out. | Exhaust |
| Give out (2) | The blast furnace is giving out a lot of heat. | Emitting |
| Give out (3) | The chairman gave out the new interest rates on HBL and FDs. | Declared/announced |
| Give over to (1) | Before exams, most students ***give over to*** their studies, which they often neglect throughout the year. | Devote oneself to |
| Give over (2) | The accused were given over to the police.<br>The working PM gave over the charge to the new state PM. | Handed over |
| Give up (1) | You should give up smoking. | Stop |
| Give up (2) | Don't give up hope in difficult times.<br>Give up bad habits if you want to improve your life. | abandon |
| | **Go** | |
| Go about | I hate this going about for the promotion of my book. | Move door to door. |
| Go about | A strong rumor goes about that he will leave us shortly. | spreads |
| Go abroad | I have never been abroad in my lifetime, and yet I am a refugee!<br>Mr. Das often goes abroad to attend | Away from home, especially a visit to a foreign country. |

| | | |
|---|---|---|
| | his business meetings. | |
| Go after | The soldiers went after the enemy | Chased |
| Go against | The police will go against the public interest. | Oppose |
| Go along | As you go along, it will soon become interesting. | Proceed/Continue |
| Go ahead | All arrangements are going ahead to celebrate the occasion. | Making progress |
| Go aside | Don't go aside from the path of virtue. | Deviate |
| Go at (1) | The two brothers go at each other at the slightest provocation. | attack |
| Go at (2) | They are going to complete the road in due time. | Making the best possible effort. |
| Go away | The beggar has gone away with all his belongings. | Left the place |
| Go back on/from | I cannot ***go back on or from*** my word. | Fail to keep |
| Go beyond | You should not go beyond your limits. | Cross limit/exceed |
| Go by (1) | You cannot always **go by** appearances. | Judge from /according to |
| Go by (2) | They talked of days gone by. | Past |
| Go by (3) | I will ***go by*** my teachers' advice.<br>It is a good rule to go by customs. | Follow one's advice or order |
| Go down | The sun has gone down. | Sunset |
| Go down (2) | The price of butter has gone down. | Reduced |
| Go down (3) | P. Bose goes down to the clan of Netaji. | Descend from |
| Go down with (4) | He has gone down with a fever. | Suffered from |
| Go for | He went for a scholarship here since he was a gold medalist in his graduation. | Receives |
| Go to (2) | Shall I go to a doctor? | *Fetch/bring/call.* |
| Go in for | We shall go for the next B. Sc's exam. | Sit for |
| Go in for (2) | The public will go in for the abolition of this custom. | Favor/support |
| Go off (1) | The bomb went off, and many people were injured. | Exploded |
| Go off | The party went well. | Passed |

| | | |
|---|---|---|
| (2) | | |
| Go off (3) | The pistol went off suddenly. | Was discharged |
| Go on | The meeting ***went on*** for ten minutes, and we then left the location. | Lasted for |
| Go out (1 & 2) | Go out in the sun.<br>The lamp ***went out*** after twelve minutes. | Leave the house to go in the sun. / Extinguish |
| Go over | He ***went over*** to the opposition party. | Changed side |
| Go over (2) | Please **go over** the accounts. | Examine |
| Go through | I shall go through the papers. | Examine fully |
| Go through (2) | My father went through great suffering during those twenty minutes, and he breathed his last. | Experienced |
| Go through (3) | I heard the proposal went through without any opposition. | Was accepted |
| Go up | The prices of essential commodities are going up. | increasing |
| Go upon | He does not go upon any fixed principles. | Follow |
| Go with | I'll go with you on this matter. | Agree with |
| Go without | He has gone without food for five days. | Passed without |
| | **Grow** | |
| Grow apart | The happiest couple grew apart last year. | Separated |
| Grow from SB | They have grown from each other; now, they live in two different places. | Become less close to or dependent on |
| Grow back | The plant grew back after it was trimmed. | Returned to a previous length. |
| Grow up | Grow up, man. Why cry over love and love, a meaningless game on thy earth! | To stop acting like a child. |

## H *for* 'Hand,' 'Hang,' 'Hold,' etc.

| Group Verbs | Examples | Meanings |
|---|---|---|
| Hand down | The custom has been handed down to the present generation. | Passed on to (next generation, etc.) |
| Hand in | The minister has handed in his | Tendered/given/ |

| | | |
|---|---|---|
| | resignation to the Governor.<br>He handed in the marriage proposal. | offered |
| Hand on | Hand the book to your friend. | Pass (to somebody) |
| Hand over | The accused was handed over to the police by the villagers. | Delivered |
| | **Hang** | |
| Hang about | The little child hangs about his father. | Remain close to |
| Hang about | Why do you hang about in the examination hall? | Move suspiciously close to SB. |
| Hang back | I am not here to hang back from my place. | Go back |
| Hang in | He hung his head in shame, but I was shameless! I kept my head up. | Bowed one's head |
| Hang on (1) | I do not like to hang on others for my bread. | Depend on |
| Hang on (2) | Can you hang on for a minute? | Wait |
| Hang on (3) | He hung on until we put him down. | Kept trying (to do something) |
| Hang out (1) | People hung out flags to welcome the Prime Minister. | displayed |
| Hang out (2) | We **hung out** in the boat and passed a pleasant night with a thousand stars over our heads. | To spend a long time together |
| Hangover (1) | Do not hang over the open balcony. | To bend down |
| Hangover (2) | The meeting has been hung over. | postponed |
| Hang together | You should all hang together and achieve success. | Support one another |
| Hang up (1) | A notice was hung up on the wall. | Put up/suspend |
| Hang up (2) | I cut short the telephone conversation and hung up. | Put down the receiver/ cut a call |
| Hang upon | The crowd hung upon the leader's words. | Listened attentively to |
| | **Hold** | |
| Hold back (1) | **Hold back** your wrath! It is improper to **pass over** us like that! | To stop doing something |
| Hold back (2) | • **Hold back** your weaknesses from your loved ones, and you are safe. | (hide/conceal) |

| | | |
|---|---|---|
| | • Truth can never be held back. | |
| Hold by | • Only friends are held by you during your difficult time. | Adhere to |
| Hold in | Hold in your temper. None here to bear with. | Check |
| Hold off (1) | Milo should hold off on such agitation. | Keep aloof/ maintain distance (from) |
| Hold on (1) | Please hold on for a minute. | Wait |
| Hold on (2) | The rain held on for two hours. | Continued |
| Held on (3) | Over the years, I ***held on*** to the project, and finally, it is the result. | Stuck to (something) |
| Hold on to STH | We should ***hold on to the course*** through all opposition. | Persevere/ persist, continue. |
| Hold out (1) | She always held out her helping hands to the known and the unknown. | Extended |
| Hold out (2) | The doctor held out little hope of his recovery. | Promised/assure d/gave |
| Hold up | He **held up** long hours, and we were about to lose our patience. | Delayed |
| Hold with | They hold with us in this matter. | Agree |

## K *for* 'Keep,' 'Knock,' etc.

| Group Verbs | Examples | Meanings |
|---|---|---|
| Keep away/off | Keep away from bad company.<br>Fire keeps off wild animals. | Keep aloof |
| **Keep back** | I never ***kept*** anything ***back*** from my lover. | Concealed |
| Keep down | You must keep down your anger. | Control/ suppress |
| Keep from | Keep from bad habits. | Refrain |
| Keep in | It is wise to keep in while it is lighting. | Stay indoors |
| Keep off | Alertness keeps off many dangers. | Wards off |
| Keep on | Keep on. You must reach your goal.<br>The fire will keep on till tomorrow. | Continue (until) |
| **Keep out** | I was kept out of the business. | Put me outside/ deny entry/ shut me out from |
| Keep to | You should always keep to your principles. | Adhere to |
| Keep under | Please keep your temper under control. | Keep in check |
| Keep up | Skipper Cook always kept up the pressure on the Indian team. | Maintained |

| | | |
|---|---|---|
| Keep up with | You must keep up with the changing world.<br>Can they ***keep up with*** us anymore after the incident? | adjust with |
| | **Knock** | |
| Knockdown | He was knocked down by a taxi. | Hit by |
| Knockdown | The building was knocked down. | Destroyed/ Broken down |
| Knock off | The workers usually knock off at five o'clock. | Stop work |
| Knock off | The shopkeeper will knock off a thousand rupees if you want to buy Peter's book. | Deduct |
| Knock out | Mary Kom knocked out her opponent in the next two rounds. | Defeated |
| Knock out | I was knocked out by the news. | Overwhelmed |
| Knock sb up | Please knock me up at five O'clock. | Make wake up |
| Knock up sth | Mother knocked up a meal for us. | Prepared hurriedly |
| Knock up | He was knocked up after five hours of work. | Tired/ exhausted |

## L *for* 'Lay,' 'Let,' 'Live,' 'Look,' etc.

| Group Verbs | Examples | Meanings |
|---|---|---|
| Lap sth up | It's a terrible movie, but audiences everywhere are lapping it up. | Accept or receive sth with great enjoyment. |
| Lap sth up | The calf lapped up the bucket of milk. | Drink all of STH with great enjoyment. |
| Lapse into | She lapsed into silence again.<br>The patient lapsed into a Coma soon after the accident. | Gradually pass into a worse state/condition. |
| Lark about | They larked about the last few months and are now complaining about their poor results. | Enjoyed or spent time in silly ways |
| Lash out at | Maizie suddenly lashed out at the boy without any provocation. | Suddenly hit somebody or sth. |
| Lash out at | In an article, Peter lashed out at his critics. | To criticize bitterly / in an angry way |
| Laugh at sb | The experts laugh at my accent, but I don't care. I ignore them always. | Mock/ make fun of/with/ignore |

| | | |
|---|---|---|
| | She laughed at me and went away. | |
| Laugh off / Laugh away | • I ***laughed off*** his suggestion of my resignation from the post.<br>• When something is likely to be beyond your patience, learn to laugh it away. | Didn't take it seriously. |
| | **Lay** | |
| Lay about | She began to lay about him in anger. | Deal blows/ rebuke/scold. |
| Layby/in | Lay something by for the future. | *save* |
| Lay down | Our freedom fighters laid down their lives for the cause of the country's liberation. | Sacrificed |
| Lay down (2) | No such rules are laid down in the book of the Constitution. | Written |
| Lay in/by/up | Hoarders laid in food for the future. He laid up enough for the future. | Store/ save |
| Lay off | Some workers were laid off for their agitation. | suspended |
| Lay on (1) | The mother laid her hand on her son's head. | Put (on) |
| Lay on (2) | Taxes at the highest rate were laid on liquid. | *Impose on* |
| Lay out | He laid it all out in the business. | Expanded |
| Lay out (2) | The garden is well laid out. | Arranged/ decorated |
| Lay up | I am laid up with a fever. | Confined to bed |
| | **Let** | |
| Let sb down (1) | The machine won't let it down. | Fail to help or support |
| Let sb/sth down (2) | Edith speaks French fluently, but her pronunciation lets her down. | Make sb/sth less successful than it should be |
| Let sb in | What left her in this situation? | Make someone involved in |
| Let in | Let him in. | (allow sb to enter) |
| Let sb off | Let her off all these. / I **refuse for her to fall into** the situation. It is my problem. Let me handle this alone. | Refuse one to fall into (a situation) |
| Let sb off | She was let off with a warning. They were our cousins. They let us off lightly. | *Release with or without punishment* |
| Let | • Being her friends, it is our | To make SB not |

| | | |
|---|---|---|
| someone out of | business to let her out of this situation.<br>• Counselling is very important to help her out of her worst condition. | feel alone in/ help someone to come out of depression |
| Let out | Suddenly, she let out a scream of terror. A long snake was facing her eyes. | *started* |
| Let up | The pain finally let up. | To become less strong |
| Let up (2) | We mustn't let up now. | To make less effort |
| | **Live, Look** | |
| Live up to | The machine does not ***live up to*** my expectations. | Work/meet (expectations) |
| Look for | Charlotte is looking for a house in the new town. | Searching for/looking for |
| Lok after | Parents look after their children out of love. | Take care of |
| Look at | Look at the birds sitting on the tower. | See |
| Look down upon/at | • He **looks down at** them as if they were his eternal slaves, and he is the Lord, equal to God.<br>• Don't look down upon the poor. | Humiliate /deride |
| Look for | We looked for better treatment from your son-in-law | Expect sth |
| Look for (2) | I am looking for the file with a yellow cover. | Searching for |
| Look forward to | We were looking forward to our uncle's visit during that time. He brought gifts and blessings for us all. | Expecting with pleasure (for) |
| Look in | I shall look in his house when I pass by his. | Pay a short visit. |
| Look into | Don't worry. I'll look into the matter soon. | Enquire/ investigate |
| Look on/ upon (1) | We looked upon you only as our well-wishers, but we were wrong. | regarded |
| Look out on/at (2) | The house ***looked out on*** the river.<br>The balcony ***looks out at*** the river. | Face to |
| Look for | The police were looking for the criminal.<br>The eagle is looking out for prey. | Watch/search for |

| | | |
|---|---|---|
| Look over | The authority reviewed his application and finally sanctioned his leave for two months. | examined |
| Look through | Please look through the letter and say where there are mistakes. | Review/examine carefully |
| Look to (1) | Look to your affairs. | Attend |
| Look to (2) | I look to you for help. | Rely on |
| Look up (1) | Pamela **looked up** and asked nothing. | Saw up |
| Look up (2) | Prices of all things, including essential commodities, have been looking up for a few months, and there is no additional income or DA. | Increasing /rising |
| Look up (3) | Please look us up while returning from London. | Visit |
| Look up (4) | Look up the nearest meaning of the word in the dictionary. | Find out |
| Look up (5) | After a dull period, Peter's business is looking up. | improving |
| Look up to | I look up to him as my elder brother. | respect |

## M for 'Make,' 'Move,' etc.

| Group Verbs | Examples | Meanings |
|---|---|---|
| Make after | The Royal Bengal tiger ***making after*** the deer was a terrible sight on our last trip to Sundarbans. | chase |
| Make away with | Farah ***made away with*** her own life. | destroyed |
| Make of | What do you make of the words? | Understand |
| Make off | The new bride made off with all the ornaments in the house. | Escaped |
| Make out | I could not make out what he said. | Understand |
| Make sth over | The principal made the charge over me. | Hand over sth upon |
| Make to | I made it to Delhi, but then I had to call off. I got down at Kanpur Station to return. | Started a journey for |
| Makeup (1) | Who makes up this loss? | Compensate |
| Makeup (2) | Two more boys will make up the team. | Complete |
| Make up a quarrel (3) | We made up our quarrel. | Develop understanding |
| Makeup (4) | They made up their minds to return. | decided |
| Move around to | Employees of the Central Government have no fixed place to live; they ***move*** | Relocate to |

***around to*** different places.

## P *for* 'Pass,' 'Pick,' 'Pull,' 'Put,' etc.

| Group Verbs | Examples | Meanings |
|---|---|---|
| **Pass away (1)** | The clouds have passed away. | dispersed |
| Pass away (2) | My old grandfather died last week. | Died |
| Pass by (1) | We pass by her house every day. | Go by |
| Pass by (2) | We should not ***pass by*** our youngsters' faults. | Overlook /ignore |
| Pass off (1) | The train has passed off. | Ceased gradually |
| Pass off (2) | He should be punished for trying to pass off false coins. | Deceive with |
| Pass off well | The ceremony passed off well. | Was a success |
| Pass off worse | The ceremony passed off worse. | Was unsuccessful |
| Pass on to | Let us ***pass on to*** another subject. | Proceed |
| Pass over | My claim was passed over. | Neglected/turned down |
| Pass through (1) | Crude oil passes through the pipe. | Goes through |
| Pass through (2) | The crew of the boat **passed through** terrible suffering. | (underwent)/ experienced |
| | **Pick** | |
| Pick at/on | Why do you always pick at me? | Find fault with |
| Pick out (1) | • Can you pick out the adverbs in the following sentences?<br>• Can you pick out the culprits in the gathering?<br>• **Pick out** the correct word from the given options and fill in the blanks. | Identify /choose |
| Pick out (2) | He picked up Italian tunes on the piano. | Played |
| Pick up (1) | Where did you pick up your English? | Learn |
| Pick up (2) | The smugglers were picked up by the police. | Arrested |
| Pick up (2) | Do you pick up the bags from my aunt on your way back? | Collect (from) |

| | | |
|---|---|---|
| Pick up (3) | I asked her to pick me up on her way home. | To give a lift |
| Pick up (4) | The share price has failed to pick up over the past days. | Improve in (business) |
| Pick up (5) | Where did you pick up malaria? | Affected by |
| Pick up (6) | Suddenly, the car picked up speed and disappeared from our sight. | Gathered |
| Pick up (7) | Our TV cannot pick up all these channels. We don't have cables. | Receive |
| Pick up (8) | I fell ill during COVID-19 but soon picked up. | Recovered |
| | **Others** | |
| Point out | He **pointed out** his views to the audience and secured victory in the upcoming election. | presented |
| | **Pull** | |
| Pull at | The workers are pulling at the heavy machine. | Trying to remove |
| Pull apart | Failing to yield to me, they started pulling me apart. | Criticize unfavorably |
| Pull down (1) | The municipal authority decided to ***pull down*** the old buildings in the locality to prevent further loss of life. | Demolish |
| Pull down (2) | He looks much pulled down. | Lowered in health or spirit |
| Pull in (1) | He is pulling in a lot of money, publishing new books every day. | Earning |
| Pull in (2) | He was pulled in by SEBI for questioning. | Detained/Arrested |
| Pull in (3) | The train pulled in on time. | Entered the platform |
| Pull off (1) | Pull off the cover and see what's in. | Remove |
| Pull off (2) | Our team pulled off a brilliant victory. | achieved |
| Pull out of (1) | The train pulled out of the station. | Left |
| Pull out of (2) | He was pulled out of difficult situations. | Come out from |
| Pulled out from behind | The lorry pulled out from behind the car. | Over crossed |
| Pullover | The driver **pulled over** the bus at the last second and saved us all. | Stop sth safely |

| | | |
|---|---|---|
| Pull through (1) | He is having great difficulty, but will pull through if we offer him a little help. | overcome |
| Pull through (2) | He was critically ill but has pulled through. | Recovered |
| Pull together | It will be done in a week if we pull it together. | Working in harmony |
| Pull up (1) | I pulled up, and I saw a traffic police officer waving his hands. | Stopped |
| Pull up (2) | He was pulled up for his misbehavior. | Reprimanded /scolded |
| Pull up (with) | Initially, he was trailing, *but soon*, he pulled up with others. | Improved relativity |
| | **Put** | |
| Put about | I hear many stories that are put about. | Spreading rumors |
| Put across | Jacob failed to put across his views to the commission. | Communicate successfully |
| Put aside (1) | We all need to put aside some amount of money for future use. | Save |
| Put aside (2) | Put aside your work and listen to me. | Stop sth for a time. |
| Put away (1) | Put away enough money for your son's education. | Lay aside/ put aside/ save |
| Put away (2) | I tried a lot but had to put away the idea of buying a car. | Give up/ abandon |
| Put away (3) | The patient was suffering, *and finally*, he had to be put away with legal permission. | Put death |
| Put back | Put the book back in its proper place. | Restore |
| Put by | Ants put by some food for the winter. Why shouldn't we? | store/accumulate |
| Put down (1) | The rebellion can't be put down by the govt. | Suppressed |
| Put down (2) | Put down only the first and second names according to the group event. | Write |
| Put forth (1) | I put forth all my energy into this task and could complete it in seven days. | Exerted |
| Put forth (2) | Trees put forth new leaves in the rainy season. | Generates |
| Put | One member of the house put | Introduced |

| | | |
|---|---|---|
| forward | forward a proposal for consideration. | |
| Put forward (2) | Dr. R.D. ***put forward*** a new theory on solar energy that could bring about a revolution. | Proposed/discovered. |
| Put in (1) | I have ***put in*** my claim to the commission. | Submitted |
| Put in (2) | Mr. Dutta has put in twenty years of teaching service. | completed |
| Put in (3) | I could not put in a word among them. | Utter a word/ say sth. |
| Put in sth for sb (4) | Please, put in a good word for me. | Plead on behalf |
| Put off (1) | The meeting was put off. | Postponed |
| Put on (1) | Put on your dress, we'll go out for a long drive. | wear |
| Put on (2) | You needn't put on a gentleman's. | disguise |
| Put on (3) | The blame was put on me. | thrushed upon |
| Put on (4) | He has put on much weight.<br>Peter and Om put on ninety runs. | added |
| Put out (1) | The fire brigade team successfully put out the fire. | Extinguished |
| Put out (2) | The death of the General put out the soldiers. | Dishearten |
| Put out (3) | He is a good man. He always puts out his hand to others. | Extends/Offers help |
| Put out (4) | He put out his hand to take the book from the table. | Stretched out |
| Put out (5) | The eyes of Pithwiraj Chowhan were put out in the camp of enemies. | Taken out /drawn out |
| Put through (1) | The task was put through twelve months. | Carried out |
| Put through (2) | After many attempts, the Internet connection was put through. | Established /run through |
| Put through (3) | The trainers at the Military Academy had to ***put through*** rigorous schedules. | Adhere to |
| Put up (1) | Rahul Dravid was a dependable player who could put up stiff resistance against rough bowlers in Test matches. | give |
| Put up (2) | A notice regarding this will be put up soon. | Hung up |

| | | |
|---|---|---|
| Put up (3) | Put up a fence around the garden. | raise |
| Put up (4) | I am putting up with my friend. | Staying for some time |
| Put up with | No one can put up with such behavior. | tolerate |

## R for 'Run,' etc.

| Group Verbs | Examples | Meanings |
|---|---|---|
| Run about | The children started to run about in great panic. | Hurry from one place to another. |
| Run across | I ran across my old friend at the ceremony after a decade. | Met by chance |
| Run after | The police ran after the thief; they caught and carried him by the neck and shoulder. | Pursued |
| Run after (2) | Do not run after money, but who listens to the words? | Pursuit/hunt for |
| Run along | Now, children, run along! | Be off/leave/go away |
| Run at | The tiger runs at the deer. | Chase |
| Run away | Leo ran away and joined the army. | Left home |
| Run away with | The dog ran away with a piece of meat. | Fled with /stole |
| Run away with | The business proposal will run away with a lot of money. | Lead to expense |
| Runaway | They had a runaway victory in the match. (runaway victory - an idiom) | Easy/an easy task |
| Run down (1) | The tiger ran down the fox and punished it with death. | Catch by chase |
| Run down (2) | • Mother looks very run down after working for three hours.<br>• The battery has been exhausted. | Exhausted /run out |
| Run down (3) | The man was run down by a reckless lorry on the Rajpath. | Run over down |
| Run into (1) | He ran into debt. | Fell into debt. |
| Run into (2) | The bus ran into the railing. | Collide with |
| Run into (3) | I ran into an old friend on the journey. | Met unexpectedly with |
| Run t | The publication has run to ten editions. | Continued |

| Runoff | The thief saw a policeman and ran off. | fled |
|---|---|---|
| Run on (1) | Our discussion ran on for hours. | continued |
| **Run on (2)** | The engine runs on CNG. | Work on |
| Run out | • The stock of food ran out.<br>• Water ran out of the tank.<br>• The garrison didn't surrender until provisions ran out. | Exhausted |
| Run over (1) | An old man was run over by a lorry. | Knocked down |
| **Run over (2)** | The river's water runs over its banks every year during the rainy season. | overflows |
| Run over (3) | She ran over the pages before entering the examination hall. | Glanced over hastily |
| Run through | Bullets ran through the body of the escaping terrorist. | Pierced |
| Run through (2) | I ran through the book and bought one for myself. | Examine quickly |
| Run through (3) | Most of us run through our fortunes to get a chance at a government appointment. | Use up /waste |
| Run to | The money required for the promotion *runs to* a few lakhs of rupees. | amount |
| Run up (1) | The boys ran up a flag on the pole. | Hoisted |
| Run up (2) | Our long stay at the Daman Diu Hotel ran up a big bill. | Caused to grow quickly |
| Run up (3) | The price of petrol rose to Rs 112. This is the third time within a month. | increased |
| Run upon (1) | The cyclist ran upon the lamp post and broke his thin helmet. | Collided with |
| Run upon (2) | I ***ran upon*** a new idea to publish multiple booklets on English Grammar to make them more accessible. | Be engrossed with/ came up with |

## S *for* 'See,' 'Send,' 'Set,' 'Stand,' etc.

| Group Verbs | Examples | Meanings |
|---|---|---|
| See About | I must see about lunch.<br>I will see about your proposal. | Prepare/consider |
| See About | He says he won't help, does he? Well, we'll soon see about that. | To deal with something/will ensure that he will… |
| See in | • I don't know what she finds in him. | Find sb/sth attractive or |

| | | |
|---|---|---|
| | • What did you see in that black spot? | interesting. |
| See off | I'll go to the station to see my friend. | To go to the station, airport, etc., to bid farewell to someone. |
| See off (2) | The home team saw off the challengers by 68 runs. | Defeat sb (in a game or fight) |
| See out | I've had this coat for years, and I'm sure it will see me out. | Run till the end of life or term/ to last longer than |
| See over | We need to review the house again before we can extend an offer. | *To review* |
| See-through | Her courage and humor saw her through | Let her be considered or allowed/ to give help or support |
| See to | Will you see to the arrangements for our next meeting? | To deal with sth. |
| | **Send** | |
| Send away/off | I'm sending the files off to my boss tomorrow. | To send data by post or mail |
| Send dow | We should send him down for his misbehavior. | Send SB to prison |
| Send for | Please ***send for*** a doctor. | Call for/summon |
| Send forth sth | He opened his mouth and **sent forth** a stream of noise. | To produce a sound to signal so that others can hear. |
| Send off | The data I sent off to my H.M. has not reached him. | Discharge by post or mail |
| Send on | We sent our furniture on an airship to Malaysia. | To **ship (send) something to a place** by ship or air. |
| Send out | Have the invitations been sent out yet? | To dispatch sth |
| Send up | Fifty boys have been sent up for higher studies in Canada. | **Refer to** for higher opportunity or prison |
| | **Set** | |
| Set about/ set forth/ /set in/ set to | Paul ***set about*** packing since morning. Sophia ***set forth*** her journey last November. /The summer vacation has ***set in*** at the institution. / Let us | To start/begin/start from |

| | | |
|---|---|---|
| | ***set to*** work at once. | |
| Set off/ set out | Nicole ***set off*** for Japan.<br>Dean ***set out*** for England last week. | Leave or start for |
| Set aside (1) | The High Court set aside the judgment of the lower court. | Canceled/put to one side |
| Set aside (2) | Mother sets aside some money to spend on those in need. | Save for the time being |
| Set aside | We need to set aside something for our bad days. | Keep apart, cast aside, or save/store. |
| Set aside | The beggar set aside a substantial amount of money through begging. | Amassed/saved |
| Set down (1) | The car set me down on the way. | Let me descend |
| Set down (2) | The police set down the woman's complaint. | Recorded |
| Set forth (1) | Leon sets forth his views in his books. | exhibits |
| Set forth/off /out | • Sophia set forth her journey last November.<br>• Nicole set off for Japan.<br>• Dean set out for England last week. | Began/Started/left for |
| Set off (2) | *He set off the drawing of Lord Shiva.*<br>He began drawing Lord Shiba. | begin |
| Set off (3) | The gains were set off against losses. | balanced |
| Set in | The rainy season has set in. | Started/begun |
| Set on/upon | The dogs were set upon the convict immorally. | Let attack |
| Set out (1) | They set out for the picnic spot early in the morning. | Start/ leave for |
| Set out (2) | He set out his goods for display. | Disperse /scatter |
| Set to/in | Let us set to work at once. | begin |
| Set up (1) | They set up a new school. | founded |
| Set (sb) up (2) | The local people set Ramesh up as their candidate in the Panchayat election. | Present/produce |
| Set up (3) | They set up a hue and cry, and a large crowd gathered. | Raised |
| Set up (4) | He set up a lawyer. | Began a profession of |
| **Stand** | | |
| Stand | All the members of the staff | Opposed |

| | | |
|---|---|---|
| against | committee stood against the principal's decision. | |
| Stand aside | Please stand aside to let the chairman pass. | Give place |
| Stand aside | He stood aside from the contest. | Took off/withdrew his name |
| Stand at | The total contribution so far stands at Rs ten thousand. | Is equal to |
| Stand by (1) | He will always stand by me. | Support |
| Stand by (2) | I merely stood by when they fought. | Was a silent onlooker/stand-off |
| Stand by (3) | In this tumultuous situation, the army is standing by to support the civil authorities. | (to be) ready |
| Stand by (4) | We should stand by our principles. | Stick to |
| Stand for | White stands for purity.<br>The letter 'L' stands for 'Learning.' | Symbolizes |
| Stand in *(for)* (1) | The hero is absent; you are asked to stand in for him. | To be substituted *(for)* |
| Stand in *(with)*(2) | This is a big amount; let me stand in with you. | Share *(*expenditure*)* |
| Stand off from | I stood off from the debate. | *Withdraw name / take off.* |
| Stand out | Her performance stood out from the rest. | Was prominent/ *conspicuous* |
| Stand over | The question will stand over for the present. | *Be left* for later settlement. |
| Stand up for | They are determined to **stand up for** their rights. | (vindicate)/support |
| Stare at | The little boy is **staring at** us. | (Looking fixedly) |

## T *for* Take, Tell, Turn

| Group Verbs | Examples | Meanings |
|---|---|---|
| Take aback | I was taken aback at the news of his insult in public. | surprised |
| Take after | The child takes after its mother. | Looks after/resembles |
| Take away | Do not take away books from the shelf. | remove |
| Take back | I will not take back my words. | Withdraw/take off |

| | | |
|---|---|---|
| Take by | The dog took the cat by its neck. | Caught by |
| Take down | Take down the names of the students | Register/write down/record |
| Take (sb) for | Everyone took him for an honest man. | Consider/regard as |
| Take from | This will take away from your reputation as a teacher. | lower |
| Take in (1) | He has taken in this plot of land for a garden. | enclosed |
| Take in (2) | I was taken in by the grocer. | cheated |
| Take in (3) | I cannot take in the meaning of the passage. | understand |
| Take in (4) | We shall take in 100 boys this year. | admit |
| Take into | Before selecting him, his health has to be taken into consideration. | sth to be considered /thought of |
| Took off | Getting back home, we ***took off*** our clothes. | Removed |
| Take off (2) | Do not take off a lame man. | mimic |
| Take off (3) | The plane will take off at 7 a.m. | Start flying |
| Take off (4) | Take your hands off my shoulders. | Remove/move off *(from)* |
| Take off (5) | The morning bus service will be taken off the route starting next week. | withdrawn |
| Take on | I decided to take on an extra job for a better livelihood. | Undertake |
| Take (sb) on | I shall take you on to table tennis, though we are two best friends at other times. | Accept as an opponent |
| Take out | Take out the aching tooth. | remove |
| Take over | The new president will take over the government's charge next month in November. | Accept |
| Take to (1) | The young boy has taken to drinking recently. | (been) addicted to |
| Take to (2) | I took to the boy from the beginning. | Became fond of |
| Take up (1) | He took up my case. | Adopted/accepted |
| Take up (2) | Mr. Peter took up the problem to solve it. | Undertook/ received |

| | | |
|---|---|---|
| Take up (3) | The car takes up too much place. We will replace it with a mini one. | occupies |
| Take up (4) | I shall take the matter up with the principal, and let's see what can be done. | Present /produce |
| Take up with | I was taken up with a book. | Absorbed in |
| Take upon | He took upon himself the burden of the family. | Took responsibility |
| Take (STH) with | He takes a folding chair with him wherever he goes. | carry |
| | **Tell** | |
| Tell against | The evidence was told against the accused. | *Prove one is guilty or responsible for* |
| Tell off | The teacher told him off for quarreling with his classmates. | Spoke angrily/rebuke |
| Tell on/upon | Smoking started to affect his health. | Affect |
| | **Turn** | |
| Turn about | The boys turned about and hurried for home. | Canceled *(a program)* |
| Turn against | I do not know why he turned against me. | Became hostile to |
| Turn away (1) | The sight pained me, and I turned away. | Turned my face |
| Turn away (2) | Turn away the idea from your mind. | dismiss |
| Turn aside | We should not turn aside from the path of honesty. | Deviate |
| Turn back | Don't turn back a beggar from your door. | Send back/reject to give anything |
| Turn down | The principal has turned down our proposal. | Reject |
| Turn in (1) | I turned in early last night. | Went to (bed) |
| Turn in (2) | We saw a hut and turned in for shelter. | Entered |
| Turn off | Turn off the switch. | *Switch off* |
| Turn on (1) | Turn on the switch. | *Switch on* |
| Turn on (2) | The case turns on his report. | Depends on |
| Turn out | The man must be turned out from here. | Driven out |

| | | |
|---|---|---|
| (1) | He is continuously making a nuisance. | |
| Turn out (2) | His story turned out to be the best in the competition. | Proved |
| Turn out (3) | The people turned out in large numbers to see the sight. | assembled |
| Turn out (4) | The mill turns out 100 pairs of clothes every day. | produces |
| Turn to | Turn to God, and He will save you. | Pray/surrender |
| Turn up | A huge crowd turned up for the match. | appeared |

## Use, Work, Write

| Group Verbs | Examples | Meanings |
|---|---|---|
| Use up | **Use up** your nails and pail to reach your goal. | (To use completely) |
| Work at | The carpenter is working at the chair. | Engaged in making |
| Work in (1) | The water has worked all around the packing box. | Penetrated |
| Work in (2) | Please try to work on a few more illustrations on the subject. | Introduce |
| Work off (1) | You must work off the accumulated work. | Dispose of/reduce |
| Work off (2) | Unless you work off your excess fat, you will fall ill. | Get rid of |
| Work on (1) | The engine works on diesel. | Runs by burning |
| Work all day and night | The workers worked all day and night, and the road was completed in record time. | Worked continuously |
| Work out (1) | Yes, finally, it **works out**. He agreed with us. | Exercises/proves successful |
| Work out (2) | I still cannot work out the sum. | solve |
| Work out (3) | I have worked out your share of Rs 10 lac. | Calculate |
| Work out (4) | Scientists have worked on a medicine to cure cancer completely. | Discover/find out |
| Work out (5) | The players are working out on the field before the match begins. | Undergoing exercise |
| Work up | The mob was worked up by his fiery speech. | excited |
| | **Write** | |
| Write down | Write down your name and address on a piece of paper. | Record |

| | | |
|---|---|---|
| Write (sb) down | You can write him down as a useless fellow. | Take him to be |
| Write off (1) | Write off your performance in the last year in the previous company. | Write a short account. |
| Write off (2) | The loss was written off. | Canceled in writing/taken as recovery not possible. |
| Write out | Please write out your name and address. | Write in full |
| Write up | He needs to write up some lines for my published books. | Write with praise |

## Exercise to Test Your Learning:

737) **Fill in the blanks with the correct phrasal verbs from the brackets:**

a) Their car ............... two kilometers away from the city. (broke down, broke in)
b) The enemy decided to _______when they couldn't fight anymore. (give away/give in)
c) They could not ______________ with each other. (get along, get together)
d) Please _______ the dictionary to find out the meaning of this word. (look up, look out)
e) I ___________________ these old photo albums when I was cleaning the house. (came forward, came across)
f) We will give the room keys when we __________ of the hotel. (check-in, check-out).
g) The minister ______________ the strike yesterday. (called off, called up)
h) The firemen had to ______ the house to rescue the children. (break into, break down)

# The Idioms or Popular Phrases

In our previous session, we learned about the seven types of phrases. Interestingly, **some phrases**, including Nominal, Relative, Adverbial, Prepositional, and Phrasal Verbs, ***are known as*** **'Idioms.'** These idioms are unique as they originate from various phrases and carry significant meanings that people have used for a long time.

## The Idioms begin with A, B, C, D, and E:

❑ **Study the Idioms & their meanings, beginning with 'A':**

1) On the question of the dowry system, we are ***at one*** point (*of the same opinion*—[complement]).
2) It is ***all one*** *(just the same)* to me whether I stay at Balurghat or go to Delhi.
3) The matter is now ***above board*** *(transparent/open-[relative phrase])*, and anybody can see and comment on it.
4) The storm broke out ***all of (on) a sudden*** *(suddenly-[adv. phrase])*.
5) I was quite ***at sea*** *(perplexed)* in this matter.
6) It was ***all but*** *(very nearly, almost)* impossible.
7) The man thinks himself to be, ***as it were*** *(like, as if)*, the lord of the earth.
8) He is ***at his wit's end*** *(completely puzzled)* in the face of trouble.
9) He is ***all in all*** *(the supreme man)* in his locality.
10) The book sale is ***at a low ebb*** *(diminishing in value)*.
11) He is not ***at all*** *(in any degree)* a scholar.
12) She comes to my house ***at times*** *(occasionally)*.

13) Do not waste time, as your examination is ***at hand*** *(close by, about to happen)*.
14) "I immediately felt ***at home*** *(feeling at ease)*."
15) The rebels surrendered ***at discretion*** *(unconditionally)*.
16) Keep bad companions ***at arm's length*** *(at a distance)*.
17) They are ***at dagger's drawn*** *(highly enraged at, in open enmity with)* with each other.
18) The cat is ***at bay*** *(in a dangerous position, in a tight corner)* in the room and turns back to attack.
19) He can teach Grammar for 36 hours ***at a stretch*** *(continue without a break)*.
20) I am ***at a loss*** *(puzzled)* and cannot escape this situation.
21) His eldest son is ***a thorn in his side*** *(a constant source of annoyance)*.
22) All the problems of Mathematics are ***at his fingers' ends*** *(ready knowledge)*.
23) These savings will be done ***in a pinch*** *(in case of emergency)*.
24) The articles in the room were ***at sixes and sevens*** *(in disheveled condition)*.

25) We reached the station ***at the eleventh hour*** *(at the last hour)*.
26) The beggar on the side is ***as good as*** *(similar to, practically no more than)* dead.
27) The life of the discoverer of an unknown land was ***at stake*** *(in a dangerous position)*.
28) He seems to be a worthless person ***at first blush*** *(at first sight)*.
29) I am afraid you two friends are ***at cross purposes (misunderstanding*** *each other)*.
30) He works ***against time*** *(with utmost speed)*.

31) He wanted that everybody would be ***at his beck and call*** *(under one's absolute control)*.
32) I can sing many Bollywood songs ***after a fashion*** *(to a certain degree, not much)*.
33) The woman is ***an ugly customer*** *(a difficult person to deal with)*.
34) This book would not be ***viable in the market (i.e., unsalable*** *due to lack of demand)*.
35) Throughout Peter's lectures, all the students were ***all ears*** *(deeply attentive)* in the seminar hall.
36) I was ***all eyes*** *(eagerly watching)* to see our C.M., but her speech was only disheartening.

37) This land is ***a bone of contention*** *(a subject of dispute)* between two brothers in the family.
38) This act is ***a dead letter*** *(no longer in force)*. Let us know the new one.
39) It is ***a long cry*** *(far away)* from Balurghat to London.
40) It is ***a far cry*** *(no easy transition)* from Capitalism to Communism.
41) The bank would not accept ***a man of straw*** *(a man of no substance, poor)* as a guarantor.
42) Unemployment is ***a hard nut to crack*** *(a complex problem to solve)*, eternal.
43) Watching short clips and videos was ***all the rage*** *(very popular)* at certain times.
44) The police are on ***a wild goose chase*** *(a fruitless search)* to catch the thief.
45) You can rely on him, as he is ***a man of his word*** *(a trustworthy person)*.
46) Only a few years ago, he entered the firm, and he is now ***at the top of the tree*** *(at the head of the profession)*.
47) This is the point ***at issue*** *(in dispute)*.
48) The death of his wife was ***a bolt from the blue*** *(a sudden, unexpected event)* to him.

### ❑ Study the Idioms & their meanings, beginning with 'B':

49) I know he will do the job ***by hook or by crook*** *(by any means)*.
50) There is ***bad blood*** *(ill feeling)* between the two families.
51) The secret of the case has been ***brought to light*** *(disclosed)* by the police.
52) ***Birds of a feather*** *(of the same nature or kind)* flock together.
53) One should know that life is not a ***bed of roses*** *(a very comfortable situation)*.
54) He ***bids fairly*** *(seems likely)* to rival his brother as a doctor.
55) He only ***beats about the bush*** *(talks irrelevantly)* in telling the story.
56) I saw him be ***beside himself*** *(out of one's mind)* with grief.
57) He visits the place ***by fits and starts*** *(irregularly)*.

58) The price of essential commodities is increasing ***by leaps and bounds*** *(very swiftly)*.
59) Mr. P was ***behind the scenes*** *(on the offside of the event)* in the successful drama.
60) ***By the bye (way)*** *(incidentally),* he asked me about the nature of my job.

61) Seeing the accident, his ***blood ran cold*** *(to be horrified)*.
62) The people of the village are, ***by and large*** *(generally speaking, on the whole)* peasants.
63) He is ***by far*** *(in every respect)* an honest man.
64) He is ***by long odds*** *(most decidedly)* the best poet in the country.
65) Mr. G is one of the ***big guns*** *(a leading personality)* of the locality.
66) The miscreants ***beat*** the traveler ***black and blue*** *(beat severely)*.
67) The chief minister took a ***bird's eye view*** *(a superficial conception)* of the flood-stricken area from a helicopter.
68) She is a ***bookworm*** *(who only reads books)* and does nothing except read.
69) He was ***brought to book*** *(given punishment)* by the headmaster for his offense.
70) The General of the enemy soldiers agreed to ***bury the hatchet*** *(cease fighting)*.
71) A modest man never ***blows his own trumpet*** *(praising oneself)*.
72) He wants to leave the place with a ***bag and baggage*** *(with all belongings)*.
73) She wastes her time ***building castles in the air*** *(indulging in doing fictitious things)*.
74) His observations on the subject were ***beside the mark*** *(irrelevant)*.
75) Corruption, as well as unemployment, is a ***burning question*** *(a matter of great importance)* today.
76) Every community has ***black sheep*** (men of evil or immoral character).
77) He ***burnt his fingers*** *(getting himself into trouble)* by helping anti-socials, providing them shelter in his house.
78) He was ***born with a silver spoon in his mouth*** *(born in wealth and luxury)*.

❑ **Study the Idioms & their meanings, beginning with 'C':**

79) His honesty cannot be ***called into question*** *(questioning the truth of a statement)*.
80) Do not ***call a person by name*** *(abuse someone)*.
81) His conduct should be ***called to account*** *(ask one to answer for misconduct)*.
82) Everybody should ***call a spade a spade*** *(to speak frankly, plainly)*.
83) The secret behind the matter has finally ***come to light*** *(publish)*.
84) Mr. Dey is ***coming to the front*** *(attain prominence)* in politics.
85) The boy ***cut a sorry figure*** (resulting in a poor result in any action or *exam)* in the final examination.

86) He ***changed color*** *(became shocked and turned pale)* when I asked him about his examination result.
87) Shiba joined the contest and ***carried the day*** *(succeed in a contest)*.
88) I can't ***call to mind*** *(recollect)* the girl's name.
89) It has been raining ***cats and dogs*** *(pouring heavily)* for two days.
90) His words ***cut her to the quick*** *(hurt one's feelings)*.
91) Tenida, one of Narayan Gangapadhyay's characters, used to tell ***cock and bull stories*** *(nonsense and absurd stories)*.
92) She came to me to shed ***crocodile tears*** *(a show of insincere sorrow through tears)* at my father's death.
93) Della was ***carried off her feet*** *(wild with excitement)* when she discovered a proper gift for Jim.
94) His thesis contained ***chapter and verse*** *(full and precise reference to authority)* for the new theories he discussed therein.
95) By his skill in arguing, he ***carried his point*** *(defeated the opponent in debate)*.
96) Employment is our youths' ***crying need*** (the essential) today, and every party is indifferent to it.
97) My scheme ***came to grief*** *(failed)* for want of funds.
98) You will ***come to grief*** *(be ruined)* if you follow that rogue.
99) The company's accountant was charged with ***cooking the accounts*** *(preparing false accounts)*.
100) The prince became king when he ***came of age*** *(became an adult)*.
101) Whatever he takes, he ***carries everything before him*** *(be entirely successful)*.
102) Doing so, you are only ***cutting your own throat*** *(ruining oneself)*.
103) He met me in the street and ***cut me dead*** *(made a deliberate insult by ignoring)*.
104) The journalist ***cut him short*** *(to interrupt one)* during his confession.
105) The labor dispute in the company ***came to a head*** *(reached a crisis)* this week.
106) The police ***caught a Tartar*** (encountered a person who proved *to be stronger than the first)* in the man they arrested first.
107) In the contest, he ***came off second-best*** *(was defeated)*.
108) He ***curries favor*** *(adopts mean ways to ingratiate oneself)* with wealthy relatives.

- **Study the Idioms & their meanings, beginning with 'D' & 'E':**

109) Sanskrit is a ***dead language*** *(a language out of use)* today when it should not be.
110) The soldier ***dies in the game*** *(dies fighting bravely)* against the enemy soldiers.
111) His father ***died in harness*** *(died while working)*, and he was appointed in his place.

112) In the ***dead of night*** *(midnight)*, the Prime Minister declared the country in an emergency.
113) While telling them, you should ***draw the line*** *(fix the limit)* where to end.
114) The two statements need ***to hang together*** *(to be consistent)*.
115) He is ***every inch*** *(entirely)* a miser fellow.
116) His every attempt to be a rich man ***ended in smoke*** *(failed)*.

## The Idioms begin with F, G, H, I, and J:

### ❑ Study the Idioms & their meanings, beginning with 'F':

117) How can a man of ***flesh and blood*** (human nature) endure much more than that?
118) His projects fell flat on the readers, and his speech ***fell flat*** (failed or had *no effect)* on his hearers.
119) Many people in this vast world live ***from hand to mouth*** *(live without making any savings for the future)*. If you have nothing to do, think about them.
120) He helped me many times when I needed him, and I am thinking about how to ***foot the bill*** *(to pay for it)*.
121) He left the service for good and engaged himself in writing novels.
122) Mr. Gupta ***falls foul of*** *(quarrels with)* everybody.
123) As he is a humbug, everybody ***fights shy of*** *(avoids)* him.
124) This year, the crop has ***fallen short of the*** *farmer's* ***expectations*** (can't meet expectations).
125) She was ***far and away*** *(very much)* the best of the singers who sang at the function.
126) His fame soon spread ***far and wide*** (**also:** far & near) *(everywhere)*

### ❑ Study the Idioms & their meanings, beginning with 'G':

127) The use of credit cards is ***gaining ground*** *(becoming more general and popular)* among the middle class.
128) Lately, he has been ***giving himself airs*** *(behaving arrogantly)* with everybody.
129) He has ***gotten rid of*** his unwelcome visitor (be free of).
130) He finally ***got the better of me*** *(overcame one)*.
131) He was guilty but ***got off easy*** *(got a light sentence or punishment)*.
132) He should ***not go back on*** *(fail to keep)* his word.
133) He should ***stay on*** (keep) his word.
134) Boys ***give their ears to*** *(listen to)* the teacher's lectures attentively.
135) If he does not shun his evil company, it will ***go hard on him*** *(prove a serious thing for one)*.

136) It ***was hard with us*** *(proved a serious thing for one)* to continue our studies when our father was dead.

137) She ***went out of her way*** *(took special effort and trouble)* to help the distressed.

138) Her simplicity ***goes to my heart*** *(touch one deeply)*, and then her cruelty causes bloodshed.

139) This subject is ***Greek (or Hebrew)*** *(which could not be understood)* to me.

140) In-need friends ***give you a cold shoulder*** *(treat one coldly)*, is not a friend indeed.

141) Nowadays, newspapers are primarily biased, ***giving false coloring to*** (*misrepresenting*) incidents; so, why not read them at all? Why believe them blindly?

142) She is ***a great hand at*** *(expert at)* organizing cultural programs.

143) His behavior ***gives a handle to*** *(gives a scope to)* suspicion.

144) A political leader should have the ***gift of the gab*** *(the ability to talk fluently)*.

- **Study the Idioms & their meanings, beginning with 'H':**

145) Both of your arguments should not ***hang together*** *(be consistent)*.

146) Your argument will ***hold water*** *(unsound thing; unfit for scrutiny)* in the seminar.

147) You should try ***heart and soul*** *(with sincerity)* to solve the problem.

148) Anil is ***hand-in-glove*** *(very intimate)* with his friends.

149) A wife always ***hopes against hope*** *(hope for something in a critical moment when it is difficult to manage)*, which is an eternal problem for some poor husbands who must maintain their livelihood with limited income.

150) The women raised a ***hue and cry*** *(outcry or noise)* when they saw the dacoits coming towards them.

151) He has ***hit the nail*** on the head *(say or do the right thing)*.

152) There is no ***hard and fast*** *(fixed)* rule in this matter.

153) This point will not ***hold good*** *(be applied)* in this discussion.

154) I believe that he ***has a hand in*** *(is concerned)* this matter.

155) I am tired of hearing her ***harp on the same string*** *(dwell tediously on the same subject)*.

156) Becoming ***hard of hearing*** *(somewhat deaf)* in danger of others is one of the common social diseases.

157) People generally become ***hard of hearing*** *(somewhat deaf)* in old age.

158) As a politician, he was ***head and shoulders*** *(very much)* above his contemporaries.

159) When he delivers lectures, the listeners ***hang on their lips*** *(listen eagerly)*.

160) The dishonest businessmen should be dealt with severely, but the Govt ***hangs fire*** *(hesitates)* to do so.
161) Our fate ***hung in the balance*** *(not decided).*
162) He may be a handicapped boy, but his ***heart is in the right place*** *(faithful & true-hearted).*

## ❑ Study the Idioms & their meanings, beginning with 'I':

163) The minister carried out the project ***in the teeth of*** *(in defiance of)* opposition.
164) She took my advice ***in good part*** *(without offense).*
165) I am ***in a fix*** *(in a trouble situation)* and unable to make a decision.
166) ***In fine*** *(in the conclusion),* he uttered the key point of his discussion.
167) Ultimately, Diligence will be rewarded ***in the long run*** *(finally).*
168) He jumped out of the running bus ***in the nick of time*** *(just at the right moment).*
169) The Police Inspector investigates the ***ins and outs*** *(full details of anything)* of the case.
170) He spent much time probing into the matter and lost a pretty sum of money ***in the bargain*** *(in addition).*
171) She told me that her son had gotten ***into hot water*** *(into trouble).*
172) He described the event ***in a nutshell*** *(in brief).*
173) He tried ***in vain*** *(fruitlessly)* to pass the examination.
174) He did the work ***in high spirits*** *(joyful).*
175) The color of the TV screen is ***in character*** *(similar)* to that of the Windows displays.
176) The boy is ***in the good books of*** *(a favorite with)* the class teacher.
177) That girl is ***in the bad books of*** *(not a favorite with)* her college teachers.
178) The patient should not keep the doctor ***in the dark*** (in ignorance) of their illness.
179) The game will again start at 6 p.m., and the players will practice a little ***in the meantime*** (between the times).
180) The police officer informed us that the troubled situation was ***in hand*** *(under control).*
181) A spirit of unrest is ***in the air*** *(found everywhere)* of the house.
182) The rogue murdered the man ***in cold blood*** *(deliberately and without passion).*
183) The police requested him to register his complaint ***in black and white*** *(in writing).*
184) Everybody says that his business is ***in the running*** *(good prospect in a competition).*
185) The preparation for the election is going ***into full swing*** *(in full energy).*
186) Since marriage, you are ***in bad odor*** *(in bad repute)* with my relatives.
187) She seems ***ill at ease*** *(uneasy)* now and then.
188) I repaid his insult ***in kind*** *(in the same way).*

189) Every man remains ***in a state of nature*** *(nakedly)* at birth.

# The Idioms begin with K, L, M, N, and O:

## ❑ Study the Idioms & their meanings, beginning with 'K':

190) He always keeps in touch with his ***kith and kin*** *(friends and relatives)*.
191) You cannot ***keep pace*** *(progress at an equal rate)* with me, though you may try very hard. It is called 'intelligence'.
192) He reads science journals regularly and ***keeps in touch with*** *(possesses intimate knowledge of)* the latest developments.
193) The quarrelsome woman ***kicked up a row*** *(making a great noise)* again and hit her son violently, this time to knock him down.
194) I find you ***know a thing or two*** *(to be wise or cunning)*.
195) Every time I go, she ***keeps a good table*** *(provides food luxuriously)*. Yet I don't know if it's her love or something else.
196) My poor father ***kept up appearances*** *(an upward show, but the condition is the opposite), though he earned nothing on the ocean and* died a king.
197) I could not ***keep the wolf from the door*** *(keep off starvation) and* fasted every time during the Shivaratri.
198) You can trust him; he ***knows what's what*** *(knows the ways of life, experienced)*.

## ❑ Study the Idioms & their meanings, beginning with 'L':

199) The new office accountant ***leaves no stone unturned*** *(uses all available ways)* to satisfy his superiors.
200) The leader of the thieves took the ***lion's share*** *(the major portion)* of the booty.
201) Ram, a poet, felt ***like a fish out of water*** *(in a strange situation)* when he was to assist a businessman.
202) It is heard that some ruffians ***laid their hands*** on Peter (attack and insult) while he was returning from the seminar.
203) In India, under British rule, some people always tried to satisfy the British rulers with ***loaves and fishes*** *(material benefits)*.
204) Relatives ***left*** the young boy and his mother ***in the lurch*** *(leading to difficulties)* when his father died.

## ❑ Study the Idioms & their meanings, beginning with 'M':

205) People gathered in large numbers to hear his ***maiden speech*** *(first lecture)*.
206) Rabindranath Tagore ***made his mark*** *(make oneself distinguished)* early on.

207) Now, Prabir is simply ***making money*** *(earning large sums of money).*
208) He ***made up his mind*** *(decided)* to enter into business, leaving his job with a bank.
209) He ***makes a clean breast of*** *(confesses frankly)* the unfair matter he was connected with.
210) The plan was a ***mare's nest*** *(a false belief, a worthless thing).*
211) The boy ***made light of*** *(treated lightly)* the teacher's warning.
212) The businessman ***makes the most of*** *(makes the best advantage of)* the opportunity to expand his business.
213) I am sure the boy ***means business*** *(is eager).*
214) The horror film ***makes the girl's blood creep*** *(make one horrified).*
215) He ***moves heaven and earth*** *(makes every possible effort)* to have a good job.
216) During war or such emergencies, some people always ***make a pile*** (*make a fortune*) by taking advantage of the situation.

## ❑ Study the Idioms & their meanings, beginning with 'N':

217) He will prove ***not worth his salt*** *(relatively worthless)* if he fails the examination this year.
218) He is ***not worth his salt*** *(entirely worthless)* if he fails at this juncture.
219) He visits my house now and then.
220) The singer is ***not in voice*** *(not able to sing)* because of a cough.
221) The law of capital punishment has now become ***null and void*** *(of no validity)* in most of the advanced countries.
222) Owing to a lack of funds, all their efforts were ***nipped in the bud*** (*destroyed at the root*).
223) I could not understand the subject's ***head or tail*** *(the main substance).*
224) This type of job is ***outside my line of work*** *(out of my knowledge or sphere of action).*

## ❑ Study the Idioms & their meanings, beginning with 'O':

225) His present action is not ***of a piece with*** *(pouring heavily)* his past actions.
226) This is ***a piece with*** *(in keeping with)* the rest of his conduct.
227) She has worked ***on and off*** *(at intervals)* ***for*** five years with this project.
228) She comes here ***off and on*** *(now and then).*
229) The guards were ***on the alert*** *(on vigilant).*
230) This custom is now ***out of date*** *(outdated, out of use, or not in practice).*
231) A political leader often delivers his speech ***off the top of his head*** *(extempore).*
232) The boy has become ***out of hand*** *(out of control)* of his father.
233) The boys are ***out of spirits*** *(sad),* having no job.
234) I see his behavior is really ***out of the way*** *(strange or abnormal).*

235) She went ***out of her way*** *(it took a special effort from her)* to help me.
236) He says he feels ***out of sorts*** *(ailing, sick)*.
237) My friend Ananda has poetry ***on the brain*** *(resting constantly in one's thoughts)*.
238) Democracy is ***on its last legs*** (reaching the verge of ruin) everywhere in the world due to extreme corruption from top to bottom.
239) There was a time I was, Peter was ***over head and ears*** *(entirely)* in debt.
240) His popularity is ***on the wane*** *(decreasing)*.
241) He is ***out and out*** *(completely)* a rogue.
242) ***On the whole*** *(after all),* the book is well-written.
243) The deal left him thousands of rupees ***out of pocket*** *(being a loser)*.
244) The meal we had in an inn last summer was ***of a kind*** *(of a bad kind)*.
245) It is unwise to do anything ***on the spur of the moment*** *(without deliberation)*.
246) The growing mistrust and hatred among the nations show that another great war is ***on the cards*** *(not unlikely)*.
247) She is ***on the wrong side*** *(more than)* of thirty.
248) The unsettled case of land dispute keeps the man ***on tenterhooks*** *(in a state of anxiety)*.

## The Idioms begin with P, Q, R, S, and T:

### ❑ Study the Idioms & their meanings, beginning with 'P':

249) Do not trust a man who ***plays fast and loose*** *(says one thing and does another)*.
250) The police examined the ***pros and cons*** *(in detail)* of the murder case.
251) Discipline is ***part and parcel*** *(an essential portion)* of a student's life.
252) I know Anil's nature is to ***put a spoke in another's wheel*** *(hinder one in the execution of one's plan)*.
253) This unexpected new difficulty ***put me on my mettle*** *(roused me to do my best)*.
254) When it comes to cheating, I ***put my foot down*** (take a determined step), for it is now a growing habit among men.
255) You did right ***put me in mind*** *(remind)* once again to send him an email.
256) All the members of the municipality ***put their heads together*** *(consult one another)* to discuss the problem of their locality, which is a good sign of democracy, which is now ***on the wane*** *(decreasing)***,** in danger for democracy, extreme decrying, and less co-operation.
257) I ***pay him back in his own coin*** (*treat one in the same way as they treat*), paying him not for the recharge.
258) In return for my trust, he ***played me false*** *(deceived)*.
259) He ***puts*** his newly composed grammar book ***on the market*** *(put for sale)*.
260) Kumar ***put a good face on*** *(bear up with courage)* his defeat in the war.

261) He ***pins his faith on*** *(gives full reliance upon)* women's right to education.
262). The majority often make this mistake; they ***play with fire*** *(trifle with serious matters unknowingly)* and hurt the sentiments of the minority.
263) We love to speak benevolence but hardly ***put our hands in our pockets*** *(give money to charity)*.
264) He is a straightforward man who can ***put two and two together*** *(make a correct inference)*.
265) Please don't ***put the screw on*** *(give pressure to do something)* me, let me decide what I should do in this situation.
266) If you do not appear in the examination, you will ***put your foot in it*** *(make a serious mistake)*.

### ❑ Study the Idioms & their meanings, beginning with '*R*':

267) Finally, he ***rose to the occasion*** *(making oneself ready for an important situation)* by publishing his book to achieve that goal.
268) The people ***rose in arms*** *(rise against)* against the tyrannical ruler every time.
269) My appeal for correction of the name has been put in ***red tape*** *(a hindrance to the disposal of any matter due to bureaucratic methods)*, but they didn't need any, while their typewriter input was wrong.
270) The 26th of January is a ***red-letter day*** *(memorable day, holiday)* for all Indians.
271) The dacoits were caught ***red-handed*** *(caught at the time of committing a crime)*.
272) The drivers of the distant-plying buses ***rest on their oars*** *(stop and relax during the time)*.
273) The country's ministers ignore the ***rank and file*** *(common, undistinguished people)* who send them to the cabinet.
274) He is the ***right-hand man*** *(the closest and efficient assistant)* of his chief.
275) Try to ***read between the lines*** *(realize the significance of the writing)* of the passage for précis writing.
276) During his tour to the village, he ***rubbed his shoulder*** *(came into close contact)* with the country's common people.
277) The workers work ***around the clock*** (the whole day), and we have our own buildings, shopping malls, etc.

### ❑ Study the Idioms & their meanings, beginning with 'S':

278). He is a slow coach (a lazy person), so he cannot prosper in life.
279) As a social reformer, he ***set his face against*** *(sternly opposed)* the leading parties.
280) The manager ***sent him about his business*** *(dismissively)* as he was lazy and disobedient.

281) He, being poor, has but one ***square meal*** *(whole meal)* a day.

282) Be cautious when typing to avoid a ***slip of the pen*** *(a slight careless mistake in writing).*

283) Forgive her; ***a slip of the tongue*** *(a slight careless mistake in speaking)* is her routine habit. By heart, she is a great one.

284) Should he not be punished for his ***sharp practice*** *(dishonest dealings)*?

285) I ***shook the dust off my feet*** *(departed indignantly)* from the meeting, as it seemed merely disgusting and intriguing against the headmaster.

286) A renowned novelist lives at a ***stone's throw*** *(a short distance)* from my house.

287) The people in the locality ***shook in their shoes*** *(trembling with apprehension),* seeing the army entering the village.

288) This ***speaks volumes for*** *(is abundant evidence of)* his honesty and sincere attitude to his work.

289) Though distressed, ***stick to your colors*** *(remain steady and faithful to one's principle)*, my boys.

290) Vidyasagar ***stuck out his chin*** *(showing firmness)* when introducing widow marriage in Bengal.

291) Vidyasagar was bold enough to ***stick his neck out*** *(expose oneself to harsh criticism by acting or speaking boldly)* in advocating for widow remarriage in the country.

292) Vidyasagar ***stuck to his guns*** *(maintain one's position under attack* to free society from age-old illiteracy and superstitions).

293) Every student should ***steer clear of*** *(take care to avoid)* bad company and any intoxication.

294) At this hour of crisis, it is no good ***splitting hairs*** *(quarreling over trifling points).*

295) He has nothing to boast of, yet he is ***swollen-headed*** *(conceited).*

296) He ***serves his time*** *(going through an apprenticeship)* at Kolkata Medical College and expects to become a fully qualified doctor soon.

297) I ***showed him my hand*** *(to disclose one's plan of action)*, expecting his cooperation or at least encouragement, but it happened elsewhere.

298) Don't trust one who doesn't stick at anything (unsteady or undetermined).

299) This occupation has ***stood me in good stead*** *(proved useful).*

300) It ***stands to reason*** *(an undoubted fact)* that a rich person can seldom be a man of outstanding creative genius.

301) Now that I have lost all my power and money, he is ***showing his teeth*** *(in a threatening mood).*

302) I ***smell a rat*** *(have reason to suspect)* in his uncalled-for beneficence.

303) On the villagers' approach in groups, the dacoits ***showed a clean pair of heels*** *(ran away).*

304) She ***stood her ground*** *(remained undisturbed)* against all adverse situations.

305) His ***stars are in the ascendant*** *(fortune favors).*

306) The news of the death of a popular leader ***spread like wildfire*** *(spread rapidly)*.

307) She ***strained every nerve*** *(made utmost effort)* to nourish her fatherless child.

308) ***Sitting on the fence*** *(between two opinions and hesitating about which side to join)* is now a general trend among politicians.

309) He dreams of ***setting the Ganges on fire*** *(or hopes for a surprising thing)*.

- **Study the Idioms & their meanings, beginning with '*T*':**

310) Despite all his brags, he had ***to eat humble pie*** *(to apologize humbly, to yield under humiliating circumstances)*.

311) Take care of what you say! You will have ***to eat your words*** *(retract your statements, take back what you have said)*.

312) I am prepared ***to meet you halfway*** *(come to a compromise with you.)*

313) It is silly ***to meet trouble halfway*** *(i.e., anticipate it, worry about it before it comes)*.

314) The cost of living has increased so much that he finds it difficult ***to make both ends meet*** *(to live within his income)*.

315) He ***took exception to*** *(object to)* my remark the other day.

316) He wants ***to pay off old scores*** *(to take revenge)* and be satisfied.

317) A sentimental person ***takes*** everything ***to heart*** *(to be deeply affected)*.

318) At the leader's encouraging words, his followers ***took to heart*** *(to take courage)*.

319) Seeing the police coming, the thief ***took to his heels*** *(ran away)*.

320). The student was ***taken to task*** (rebuked, scolded*)* for his misconduct toward junior teachers.

321) Why do people ***turn a deaf ear to*** *(do not hear from)* a person in danger? Just look at yourself, and you'll get your answer.

322) He has ***turned over a new leaf*** *(changed the course for a better life)* by publishing his book.

323) He who stays by ***through thick and thin*** *(under all conditions)* is a real friend.

324) My colleagues ***throw cold water*** *(discourage showing indifference)* on my new plan to publish a new book on composition after the book on grammar.

325) You can ***turn your hand to*** *(undertake a new job)* any work that suits you better.

326) He ***turns*** his new deal ***to account*** *(make a profit)*.

327) He was pacing ***to and from*** *(here and there)* in the room.

328) Unemployment and corruption are ***the order of the day*** *(the present state of things)*.

329) He translated the Bengali passage into English ***to the letter*** *(to every detail)*.

330) We must fight ***tooth and nail*** *(with all our might)* to eradicate illiteracy from our country.
331) The villagers voted ***in his favor***, without exception.
332) He ***turns up his nose*** *(shows disdain)* at your property earned by unfair means.
333) He has ***too many irons in the fire*** *(engaged in many jobs at the same time)*, yet he proceeds steadily.
334) We need guards who are ***true to their salt*** *(faithful to the employer)*.
335) This dress suits her ***to a T*** *(correctly)*.
336) ***The long and the short of*** *(the whole subject in a few words)* what I want to say is that I shall not join you in your new business.
337) The new officer wants ***to take stock of*** *(to look at carefully)* the whole matter before starting the investigation.
338) The explorers ***took life in their hands*** *(faced great risk)* at every step of their journey in the unknown region.
339) His friend ***took the wind out of his sails*** *(make one's action ineffective by anticipation)* in his work of publishing an English Grammar book.
340) The man, unable to work, wants ***to rest on his laurels*** *(to retire)*.
341) He has ***made good the loss*** *(to compensate for the loss)*.
342) I know ***the ins and outs*** *(full details)* of his present deplorable condition.
343) He has become rich and now ***takes things easy*** *(do not labor)*.
344) Peter profited in the business by ***taking a leaf from his friend's book*** *(imitate one or profit by one's example)*.
345) While giving him punishment, you should ***take into account*** *(consider)* also his noble deeds.
346) You should attempt ***this thing*** *(the proper thing)*.
347) I ***tried my hand*** *(made an effort)* at writing science fiction at late hours, and I failed.
348) It is difficult for a poor man like Peter ***to keep his head above water*** *(to keep out of debt)*.
349) Her manager was a wicked man ***to the backbone*** *(to the core)*.
350). He ***took my breath away*** *(to surprise me very much)* when he gave me news of his becoming a gold medalist in his doctorate.
351) Try your best ***to crow over*** *(to win over)* your opponent.
352) You should not expect me ***to see eye to eye*** *(in complete harmony)* with you in this work.
353) She is a habitual liar, so everybody ***takes*** her words ***with a grain of salt*** *(doubt)*.
354) This shoe fits you, madam, ***to a nicety*** *(exactly)*.
355) Don't ***thrust your nose into*** *(interfere unnecessarily)* anybody's affair.
356) He has ***two strings to his bow*** *(two sources of income to live on)*: working in a government office and privately practicing Homeopathy.
357) The patent has ***turned the corner*** *(passed over the crisis)*.
358). He talks sharply (only about business), and nobody likes him.

# The Idioms begin with U, V, W, X, Y, and Z:

- **Study the Idioms & their meanings, beginning with *'U'* & *'W'*:**

359) A business has its ***ups and downs*** *(rise and fall).*
360) I asked the shopkeeper to give me a dictionary book with meanings ***up to date (as of*** *the present time).*
361) Your performance was not ***up to the mark*** *(equal to the standard).*
362) The book that he requires is ***under his nose*** *(very close to one's presence)*, but being absent-minded, he cannot see it.
363). The lecture hall is filled ***to the brim*** with an audience.
364) Consult with him; he has ***well-balanced*** *(reasonable)* opinions.
365) My proposal was accepted ***with one voice*** *(unanimously).*
366) A wearer knows ***where the shoe pinches*** *(where the trouble lies).*
367) The king ruled his subjects ***with a high hand*** *(with oppression).*
368) He did the job ***with might and foremost*** *(with the utmost strength).*
369) He ***washes his hands of*** *(refuses to do anything more)* the whole matter.
370) I can accept your statement ***without reserve*** *(full)* if you add this point.
371) Gandhiji welcomed Louis Fischer to his Ashram with open arms (an open heart, a *warm welcome).*
372) Sachin ***won his laurels*** *(acquired a distinction or glory)* in cricket.
373) As a pop singer, she ***won her spurs*** (acquired her reputation).
374) The Indian Railway soon became a ***white elephant*** *(a costly, unprofitable object)* to the Govt after the Indian Airlines.
375) At the battle of Marengo, Napoleon was ***within an ace of*** *(on the point of)* defeat. (i.e., he was very nearly defeated.)

# The Use of Prepositions with Other Words

1. Certain ***Nouns, Adjectives, Participles***, & ***Verbs*** are always followed by particular Prepositions.

## Conjugation of Prepositions with Nouns or Gerunds:

### Nouns with 'for'

A. Certain ***Nouns*** which are followed by the '***for***' Preposition:

1) She had ***affection for*** none. Don't cherish ***anxiety for*** others.
2) I sought an ***apology for*** my fault, yet she hardly forgave me for my innocent affair with the girl.

3) I had no ***appetite for*** your love, yet you pushed me a thousand times into the affair. Wow, how noble I was!!
4) The public has an insatiable ***appetite for*** scandal.
5) You have no ***aptitude for*** this job. I am sorry.
6) Why do you ***blame*** it ***for***? The tank has no ***capacity for a*** thousand liters.
7) We urgently ***need*** candidates ***for*** the recruitment. Make the process fast, C.M.'s order.
8) She was a noble and kind woman who had ***compassion*** even ***for*** a dead rat, but not for her husband.
9) They sought ***compensation for*** their loss; we had hardly anything.
10) Your ***contempt for*** women will make you soon hateful among netizens.
11) There is still no ***cure for*** the common cold.
12) Little Jack proved quite a ***match for*** the giant.

❑ And thus, *craving, desire, esteem, fitness, fondness, guarantee, leisure, liking, match, motive, need, opportunity, partiality, passion, pity, prediction, pretext, relish, remorse, reputation, surety, etc.*— all the nouns take ***'for'*** preposition after them.

13) I have a ***craving for*** chocolate every night after dinner.
14) Her ***desire for*** adventure led her to travel the world.
15) He has a deep ***esteem for*** his mentor, who has guided him throughout his career.
16) She is working hard to improve her ***fitness for*** the upcoming marathon.
17) His ***fondness for*** classical music is evident in his extensive vinyl collection.
18) The company offers a ***guarantee for*** its products, ensuring customer satisfaction.
19) I always make ***time for*** leisure activities to maintain my mental well-being.
20) She has a strong ***liking for*** Italian cuisine and often tries new recipes.
21) They are looking for a perfect ***match for*** their start-up project.
22) Understanding his ***motive for*** moving might help us support him better.
23) There is an increasing ***need for*** more sustainable energy solutions.
24) This internship provides a valuable ***opportunity for*** growth and learning.
25) She has a ***passion for*** painting, and it shows in her beautiful artwork.
26) I felt a sense of ***pity for*** the stray dog that wandered into our yard.
27) The weather service issued a ***prediction for*** rain this weekend.
28) He used the meeting as a ***pretext for*** visiting his old colleagues.
29) My grandmother had a ***relish for*** gardening and spent hours tending to her plants.
30) He expressed his ***remorse for*** his actions and wanted to make amends.
31) The restaurant has a ***reputation for*** serving the best pizza in town.
32) She spoke with ***surety for*** her project, confident in its success.

## Nouns with 'with'

B. Certain *Nouns* which are mainly followed by '***with***':

33) I have no ***acquaintance with*** this man.
34) Regarding this, the country has an ***alliance with*** Japan.
35) I hate ***bargains with*** beggars. Do you have any ***comparison with*** the two?
36) If we had this ***conformity with*** the declaration by the Government, but alas, we are left with none.
37) What is your ***enmity with*** him? Resolve that soon.
38) She had ***intercourse with*** her boyfriend, she proudly admitted.
39) Why is this ***intimacy with*** him and all these behind your husband?

## Nouns with 'of,' 'about,' 'in,' and 'on.'

C. Certain nouns are mainly followed by ***'of,' 'about, '*** and ***'in.'***

40) The celebrated grammarian Patanjali was a ***contemporary of*** Pushyamitra Sunga.
41) I give ***assurance of*** surety, no problem. He was ***in charge of*** the police station.
42) She fell into deep ***despair of*** losing her job, unsure of the future.
43) Pitila has ***a dislike for*** tea.
44) ***Distrust of*** humanity is a wrong idea for your existence.
45) Sorry, sir, I have no ***experience in*** teaching; see others.
46) ***Failure of*** the goal to give a lecture!
47) Keep an ***eye on*** her progress and inform us in time.
48) Do you have any ***proof of*** my guilt? If not, think a thousand times before making a decision.
49) They may have a ***want of*** money, but they are not a scoundrel.
50) The President ***called for*** an immediate ***cessation of*** hostilities among the communities in West India.
51) They doubt our projects and schemes. They have ***doubts about*** our schemes.
52) You'll get a 5% ***concession on*** the total price of this item.

## Nouns with 'to', 'toward', and 'from'

D. Certain *Nouns* which are mainly followed by '***to***'

53) We have no ***access to*** the basement.
54) Then, the people celebrated Charles I's ***accession to*** the throne.
55) He affirmed his ***allegiance to*** the President.
56) It is an ***alternative to*** that medicine.

57) In my youth, I had the ***ambition to*** become a writer. Alas! I could become none.
58) Do you have an ***antidote to*** that disease?
59) The citizens grow ***antipathy to*** (also: towards) the new Act of Government.
60) We shouldn't ***approach*** this proposal. It seems ***risky for*** us.
61) The director has given her ***assent to*** the proposal.
62) The mother has always had a special ***attachment to*** her elder child.
63) Please give your ***attention to*** me.
64) He made a ***complaint to*** the principal, ma'am, about her roommate being drunk.
65) The director has given her ***consent to*** the proposal.
66) It was a ***disgrace to*** his dignity, and he showed his power over us.
67) ***Encouragement to*** the child is the duty of every parent.
68) It was an ***exception to*** his nature, or he was very fine, cool, and temperate.
69) She would be engrossed in ***listening to*** the news on the TV.
70) I have no ***relation to*** her anymore. We have departed since last year.
71) He traces his ***lineage to*** the Maurya kings.
72) We had no ***enmity toward*** anyone.
73) We had no ***hostility toward*** anyone.

❑ And thus, *incentive, indifference, invitation, key, leniency, likeness, limit, menace, obedience, objection, obstruction, opposition, postscript, preface, reference, repugnance, resemblance, sequel, submission, succession, supplement, temptation, traitor*— all the nouns take *'to'* preposition after them.

74) The company offered a financial ***incentive to*** employees who exceeded their sales targets.
75) His ***indifference to*** the team's struggles frustrated his coach.
76) She received an ***invitation to*** the gala and was excited to attend.
77) Trust is the ***key to*** a successful relationship.
78) In his rulings, the judge showed ***leniency to*** first-time offenders.
79) Her facial features show a surprising ***likeness to*** her father.
80) There is no ***limit to*** the potential of young minds.
81) Climate change poses a serious ***menace to*** global ecosystems.
82) His ***obedience to*** the rules earned him the respect of his peers.
83) Her ***objection to*** the proposal was based on concerns for public safety.
84) They faced an ***obstruction to*** their plans due to regulatory issues.
85) The senator's strong ***opposition to*** the bill was evident in her speech.
86) His ***partiality to*** that team is well-known among his friends.
87) The author added a ***postscript to*** clarify certain points in the book.
88) The ***preface to*** the novel provides insight into the author's inspiration.
89) The professor included a ***reference to*** relevant studies in her lecture.

90) His ***repugnance to*** unfair practices made him an advocate for transparency.
91) There is a striking ***resemblance to*** her sister, making them look remarkably alike, as if they were twins.
92) The ***sequel to*** the blockbuster movie was highly anticipated by fans.
93) Her ***submission to*** the competition was praised for its creativity.
94) The ***succession to*** the throne was carefully planned by the royal family.
95) The doctor recommended a ***supplement to*** enhance her nutrition.
96) He struggled with the ***temptation to*** break his diet during the holidays.
97) The spy was labeled a ***traitor to*** his country for leaking sensitive information.

E. Certain ***Nouns*** which are mainly followed by '***from***'

98) You need total ***abstinence from*** drinking if you want to live.
99) He sighed long after ***deliverance from*** sure death.
100) He traces his line of ***descent from*** the Maurya kings.

❑ **Note:** *when it means 'ancestry or family origin,' it takes* **'from'**; *but when it means a 'slope going downward,' it takes* **'to'**; *when it means 'coming or going down,' it takes* **'into'** *after it; as,*

101) There is a gradual ***descent to*** the sea.
102) The country's swift ***descent into*** anarchy was bad luck for the countrymen.
103) His ***digression from the*** main point is too disgusting to run a conversation.
104) She was given an ***exemption from*** the final examination.
105) The President is ***exempt from*** paying taxes to the government.
106) Buddhism teaches that ***freedom from*** desires will lead to ***escape from*** suffering.
107) Her ***inference from*** ignorance to knowledge is sufficient reason to give her an appointment.
108) I need some ***respite from*** this tiresome job.

## Conjugation of Prepositions with Participles or Adjectives:

## Adjectives or Participles with 'to'

*A.* Certain ***Adjectives or Participles*** that are followed by the Preposition ***'to'***

109) These computers are cheap enough to be ***accessible to*** most people.
110) It was ***adequate to*** meet our needs, but we are undone even with it.
111) The house was ***adjacent to*** the post office.
112) The true gentleman is courteous and ***affable to*** his neighbors.

113) Be ***affectionate to*** your younger brother.
114) Neither was ***akin to*** us. Everything was ***alien to*** our knowledge.
115) Still, he is ***alive to*** his citizens.
116) People who are ***averse to*** hard work generally do not succeed ***in*** life.
117) Why are you ***callous to*** everything?
118) It is ***common to*** every mortal man.
119) He is ***contrary to*** his younger brother.
120) She was ***determined to*** marry that rascal; what could we do to her poor parents?
121) It was ***due to*** his fate that he did not pass.
122) It was formerly supposed that malaria was ***due to*** poisonous exhalations.
123) The true gentleman is courteous and ***generous to*** his neighbors.
124) His works were ***ill-suited to*** his ardent and daring character.
125) Newly acquired freedom is sometimes ***liable to*** abuse.
126) The students are ***obedient to*** their teachers. It was relevant to the treaty.
127) The true gentleman is courteous and ***pleasant to*** his neighbors.
128) Dr. Sen was somewhat ***susceptible to*** flattery.

❑ And thus, abhorrent, acceptable, agreeable, amendable, analogous, applicable, appropriate, beneficial, comparable, condemned, conducive, conformable, comfortable, congenial, consecrated, contrary, creditable, deaf, derogatory, detrimental, devoted, disastrous, entitles, equal, essential, exposed, faithful, fatal, foreign, hostile, impertinent, incidental, inclined, indebted, indifferent, indispensable, indulgent, inimical, insensible, injured, irrelevant, favorable, hurtful, immaterial, hurtful, impervious, Indigenous, limited, lost, loyal, material, natural, necessary, obliged, offensive, opposite, painful, partial, peculiar, pertinent, pledged, preferable, prejudicial, prior, profitable, prone, reduced, related, relevant, repugnant, responsible, restricted, sacred, sensitive, serviceable, subject, suited, supplementary, tantamount, true, etc., — all the adjectives or participles take *'to'* preposition after them.

129) The act of pollution is ***abhorrent to*** anyone who cares about the environment.
130) Her behavior was deemed ***acceptable to*** the standards of the organization.
131) The terms of the contract were ***agreeable to*** all parties involved.
132) The proposal is ***amenable to*** suggestions from the stakeholders.
133) His situation is ***analogous to*** that of the other candidates.
134) The new rules are ***applicable to*** all employees in the company.
135) It's ***appropriate to*** dress formally for the wedding.
136) Exercise is ***beneficial to*** both physical and mental health.
137) Her achievements are ***comparable to*** those of the best athletes.

138) He felt ***condemned to*** a life of monotony.
139) A quiet environment is ***conducive to*** studying effectively.
140) This chair is ***comfortable to sit in*** for long periods.
141) He found the climate ***congenial to*** his health.
142) The temple is ***consecrated to*** the goddess of wisdom.
143) His beliefs are ***contrary to*** the mainstream opinions.
144) Creditable to: The team's effort was ***creditable to*** their dedication.
145) She remained ***deaf to*** the warnings about the storm.
146) His comments were ***derogatory to*** his colleagues.
147) Smoking is ***detrimental to*** your health.
148) She is ***devoted to*** her family and career.
149) The decision was ***disastrous to*** the company's reputation.
150) Hard work ***entitles*** *you* ***to*** the rewards you desire.
151) Their contributions are ***equal to*** those of the other members.
152) It is ***essential to*** have a backup plan in case of emergencies.
153) Children are often ***exposed to*** various forms of media.
154) He remained ***faithful to*** his commitments.
155) A lack of oxygen can be ***fatal to*** humans.
156) The concept was initially ***foreign to him.***
157) The climate was ***hostile to*** the expedition.
158) Her behavior was seen as ***impertinent to*** the guests.
159) The costs were ***incidental to*** the overall budget.
160) She was ***inclined to*** believe in the impossible.
161) I feel ***indebted to*** my parents for their support.
162) He was ***indifferent to*** the outcome of the game.
163) Water is ***indispensable to*** all forms of life.
164) His parents were ***indulgent to*** his every request.
165) The policies were ***inimical to*** economic growth.
166) He seemed ***insensible to*** the pain around him.
167) The athlete was ***injured to*** the point of losing his career.
168) His remarks were ***irrelevant to*** the discussion at hand.
169) The conditions were ***favorable to*** the team's performance.
170) Her words were ***hurtful to*** his feelings.
171) The details were ***immaterial to*** the overall argument.
172) Some jokes can be ***hurtful to*** others.
173) She seemed ***impervious to*** criticism.
174) The species is ***indigenous to*** the region.
175) The offer is ***limited to*** the first 100 customers.
176) Many traditions are ***lost to*** modern culture.
177) He remained ***loyal to*** his friends through thick and thin.
178) The evidence is ***material to*** the case.
179) It is ***natural to*** feel anxious before a big presentation.
180) It is ***essential to*** follow safety guidelines.
181) She felt ***obliged to*** help her neighbor.
182) His remarks were considered ***offensive to*** the audience.

183) The results were ***opposite to*** what we expected.
184) It was ***painful to watch*** the final moments of the match.
185) She is ***partial to*** chocolate over vanilla.
186) The behavior is ***peculiar to*** that species.
187) Her questions were ***pertinent to*** the topic being discussed.
188) The organization ***pledged to*** help the community.
189) It is ***preferable to*** arrive early rather than to be late.
190) Ignorance can be ***prejudicial to*** effective decision-making.
191) ***Prior to*** the meeting, it is ***essential to*** prepare.
192) Investments can be ***profitable for*** long-term growth.
193) He is ***prone to*** making hasty decisions.
194) The team was ***reduced to*** only six players due to injuries.
195) This topic is closely ***related to*** climate change.
196) Her experience is ***relevant to*** this position.
197) The idea was ***repugnant to*** his moral beliefs.
198) He is ***responsible to*** all shareholders of the company.
199) Access to the area is ***restricted to*** authorized personnel.
200) That site is considered ***sacred to*** the local community.
201) She is ***sensitive to*** loud noises.
202) The equipment is still ***serviceable to*** our needs.
203) The agreement is ***subject to*** further review.
204) He was well ***suited to*** the role.
205) The extra readings are ***supplementary to*** the main text.
206) His silence was ***tantamount to*** an admission of guilt.
207) She remained ***true to*** her values despite the pressure.

## Adjectives or Participles with 'in' and 'with'

B. Certain ***Adjectives or Participles*** followed by the Preposition ***'in.'***

208) He is ***absorbed in*** her thoughts. He is in love.
209) You were ***accurate in*** the calculation.
210) She was ***backward in*** class as per your class division.
211) Peter was ***correct in*** his assumption.
212) He was ***deficient in*** management.
213) We are not ***experienced in*** this field.
214) He is ***honest in*** his words; we should believe him.
215) I am not ***interested in*** cycling, but it would benefit my health.
216) How did you get ***involved in*** this thing?
217) Be ***temperate in*** thoughts and actions; success is at your feet.

- And thus, abstemious, accomplished, assiduous, bigoted, diligent, enveloped, fertile, foiled, implicated, lax, negligent, proficient, remiss, versed, etc.— all the adjectives take ***'in'*** preposition after them.

218) She was ***abstemious in*** her eating habits, choosing only healthy foods.
219) He is ***accomplished in*** multiple languages, which makes him a valuable asset to the team.
220) The student was ***assiduous in*** her studies, often spending late nights preparing for exams.
221) His ***bigoted*** views ***in*** politics alienated many of his friends.
222) She is ***diligent in*** her work, always meeting deadlines ahead of schedule.
223) The city was ***enveloped in*** mist, creating an eerie atmosphere.
224) The region is ***fertile in*** agriculture, producing a variety of crops each season.
225) He is ***lavish at*** night parties. The lavish party was ***generous in*** terms of both time and expense.
226) He was ***implicated in*** the scandal, raising questions about his integrity.
227) The company was ***lax in*** its security measures, resulting in a breach.
228) The employee was ***negligent in*** his duties,
229) She became ***proficient in*** coding after dedicating months to practice.
230) He was ***remiss in*** his duties, failing to report important findings.
231) He was ***slow in*** making decisions, always weighing his options carefully.
232) The consultant is well-***versed in*** the latest industry trends, providing clients with invaluable insights.

C. Certain ***Adjectives or Participles*** followed by the Preposition ***'with.'***

233) I am ***acquainted with*** the President; let me go in, sir, or inform him about my presence. Tell him Peter has come.
234) He was ***afflicted with*** sorrow and told us, 'No.' He is not coming with us.
235) Let's get ***busy with*** clearing up the mess on the floor.
236) He was ***contemporary with*** the dramatist Congreve.
237) The guests were ***content with*** the service.
238) Emily was ***delighted with*** her success and achievement.
239) The text color is ***contrasted with*** its background color.
240) Jayden was ***gifted with*** his remarkable I.Q.
241) It was ***infected with*** poison. He was very ***popular with*** his fans and followers.
242) Was she ***satiated with*** her desires? I am ***satisfied with*** my achievement.
243) India is a noble, gorgeous land ***teeming with*** natural wealth.

- ❑ And thus, acquainted, beset, compatible, compliant, conversant, convulsed, deluged, disgusted, drenched, endowed, fatigued, fired, infatuated, infested, intimate, invested, overcome, replete, touched, etc. — all the adjectives take ***'with'*** preposition after them.

244) I am already ***acquainted with*** the latest developments of the situation.
245) The company was ***beset with*** challenges during the merger process, making it difficult to integrate the two cultures.
246) The software is ***compatible with*** all major operating systems, allowing users to access it from any device.
247) The policy is ***compliant with*** the legal regulations.
248) All employees are required to be ***compliant with*** the new safety regulations to ensure a safe working environment.
249) Her performance was ***consistent with*** her previous results.
250) She is ***conversant with*** the latest research in artificial intelligence, which enables her to make informed decisions.
251) He was ***convulsed with*** laughter when he heard the hilarious joke shared by his friend.
252) The town was ***deluged with*** rain last night, causing many roads to close due to flooding.
253) She felt ***disgusted with*** the way the situation was handled and decided to voice her concerns.
254) The hikers returned home ***drenched with*** sweat after a challenging climb up the mountain.
255) His speech was ***dull with*** excitement, causing many to fall asleep.
256) He was ***endowed with*** exceptional musical talent, which he nurtured from a young age.
257) After hours of studying for exams, I felt ***fatigued with*** the monotony of work and ready for a break.
258) She was ***fired with*** a determination to complete the project ahead of the deadline.
259) Few things are ***impossible with*** diligence and skill.
260) He was ***infatuated with*** her charm and wit, often daydreaming about their time together.
261) The old house was ***infested with*** termites, prompting the new owner to call for immediate pest control.
262) They became ***intimate with*** each other after years of friendship, deepening their bond.
263) The new technology is ***invested with*** potential benefits that could revolutionize the industry.
264) She was ***overcome with*** joy upon hearing the news of her promotion.
265) The garden was ***replete with*** vibrant flowers, creating a stunning display in the spring.
266) He was ***touched with*** a sense of nostalgia as he walked through his childhood neighborhood.

# Adjectives or Participles with 'of'

D. Certain ***Adjectives or Participles*** which are followed by the Preposition ***'of'***

267) Deb was ***accused of*** an illegal love ***affair with*** his ex-student, Piya.
268) However, he was ***acquitted of*** all charges and sent to an asylum due to his mental health.
269) I am not ***afraid of*** you or anybody you call.
270) I was a little ***apprehensive of*** the effects.
271) ***Apprised of*** our approach, the neighborhood came out to meet their minister.
272) We were ***assured of*** the best service. Are you ***aware of*** this?
273) They were not ***cautious of*** the coming danger.
274) He should not be ***deprived of*** his rights.
275) Naples was then ***destitute of*** what are now, perhaps, its chief attractions.
276) Why are you ***envious of*** them?
277) Jawaharlal Nehru was ***fond of*** children.
278) He is a man of deep learning but ***ignorant of*** life and manners.
279) Ashoka, although ***tolerant of*** competing creeds, was personally an ardent Buddhist.

- ❑ And thus, bereft, bought, certain, characteristic, composed, confident, conscious, convicted, convinced, covetous, defrauded, desirous, devoid, distrustful, easy, fearful, greedy, guilty, heedless, informed, innocent, irrespective, productive, proud, regardless, sanguine, sensible, sick, subversive, sure, suspicious, vain, void, weary, worthy, etc.— all the adjectives take *'of' preposition* after them.

280) After the breakup, she felt completely ***bereft of*** joy.
281) He was ***certain of*** his decision to move to a new city.
282) The bright colors are ***characteristic of*** the artist's unique style.
283) The committee is ***composed of*** several experts in the field.
284) She was ***confident of*** her ability to succeed in the exam.
285) He was ***conscious of*** the time ticking away during the presentation.
286) The man was ***convicted of*** theft and sentenced to three years in prison.
287) She was ***convinced of*** her friend's innocence in the matter.
288) He was ***covetous of*** his neighbor's success and lifestyle.
289) The elderly couple was ***defrauded of*** their savings by a scam artist.
290) She was ***desirous of*** a peaceful life away from the chaos.
291) The landscape was ***devoid of*** any trees, creating a stark view.
292) After the incident, she became ***distrustful of*** strangers.

293) She was ***fearful of*** the dark and never wanted to go out alone at night.
294) She was ***jealous of*** the attention her friend received during the event.
295) The children were ***heedless of*** the warnings and ran into the street.
296) She was ***informed of*** the changes to the schedule via email.
297) He claimed to be ***innocent of*** the accusations against him.
298) They decided to proceed, ***irrespective of*** the potential risks involved.
299) The meeting was ***productive of*** new ideas and collaborations.
300) She felt ***proud of*** her accomplishments and the journey it took to get there.
301) He went ahead with his plan ***regardless of*** the consequences.
302) It would be ***sensible of*** them to prepare for any unforeseen events.
303) I'm ***sick of*** the constant negativity in the news.
304) The group's activities were viewed as ***subversive of*** the current regime.
305) I am ***sure of*** my ability to handle the upcoming challenges.
306) He was ***suspicious of*** their intentions from the very beginning.
307) She was ***vain of*** her appearance, often checking her reflection in mirrors.
308) The contract was deemed ***void of*** any legal standing.
309) He was ***weary of*** the endless debates that seemed to go nowhere.
310) Her actions were truly ***worthy of*** admiration and respect.

## Adjectives or Participles with 'for'

E. Certain ***Adjectives or Participles*** are followed by the preposition ***'for.'***

311) Every mother is ***anxious for*** her child. He is ***celebrated for*** his last song.
312) It is ***designed for*** gentlemen. I am not ***eager for*** it or anything like that.
313) He was ***destined for*** death for his continuous criminal acts.
314) We were not ***eligible for*** the recruitment, but they made it clear on our faces.
315) Mumbai is ***famous for*** its textiles. Do you think you're ***fit for*** this?
316) The Moors were ***renowned*** for their expertise in various fields.
317) It was merely his ***lame excuse for*** avoiding the meeting.
318) The gang was ***notorious for*** dacoity in that area for decades.
319) Coleridge's poetry is ***remarkable for*** the perfection of its execution.

- And thus, conspicuous, customary, eminent, good, grateful, penitent, prepared, proper, qualified, ready, sorry, sufficient, useful, jealous, etc. — all the above adjectives take ***'for'*** preposition after them.

320) The bright colors of the flowers were ***conspicuous for*** attracting the

attention of all passersby.

321) It is ***customary for*** guests to bring a gift when attending a dinner party.

322) The scholar was ***eminent for*** her groundbreaking research in environmental science.

323) Eating fruits and vegetables is ***good for*** maintaining a healthy lifestyle.

324) I am ***grateful for*** the support my friends have given me during difficult times.

325) The corporation was ***greedy for*** profit, neglecting its social responsibilities.

326) He felt ***penitent for*** his actions and sought to make amends.

327) She was well-***prepared for*** the exam after weeks of diligent study.

328) Wearing a suit was considered ***proper for*** the formal occasion.

329) He was ***qualified for*** the job due to his extensive experience in the field.

330) The team was confident in its training and ***ready for*** the challenge ahead.

331) She was genuinely ***sorry for*** missing the meeting and promised to catch up with her teammates.

332) The funds raised were ***sufficient for*** completing the community project.

333) The outfit was ***suitable for*** the occasion.

334) This tool is incredibly ***useful for*** completing carpentry tasks efficiently.

## Adjectives with 'from,' 'at,' 'about,' and 'by.'

F. Certain ***Adjectives or Participles*** also take other prepositions, like ***'from,' 'at,' 'about,'*** and ***'by.'***

335) Man is entirely ***different from*** other animals in the utter hopelessness of his babyhood.

336) The President is ***exempt from*** paying taxes to the government.

337) The doctor is ***busy at*** the moment. Gomez was ***busy at*** her work.

338) He is ***lavish at*** night parties. The lavish party was ***generous in*** terms of both time and expense.

339) I was ***ambitious about*** becoming a great author.

340) He felt ***diffident about*** his opinions in such a large group.

341) He felt ***guilty about*** his past mistakes that hurt others.

342) She remained ***sanguine about*** the outcome despite the challenges faced.

343) We are ***inspired by*** his advice.

344) They are ***surprised by*** your talent.

## Conjugation of Prepositions with Verbs:

## Verbs with 'to' and 'from'

*A.* The Certain ***Verbs*** which are in most cases followed by the Preposition ***'to.'***

345) The boarders are ***accustomed to*** rising early.
346) Camels are peculiarly ***adapted to*** life in the desert.
347) Ivory readily ***adapts itself to*** the carver's art.
348) The ancient Greeks, though born in a warm climate, seem to have been much ***addicted to*** the bottle.
349) He ***complained to*** the principal, ma'am, about her roommate being drunk.
350) Ambition does not always ***conduce to*** ultimate happiness.
351) The African elephant is now ***confined to*** Central Asia.
352) I am ***indebted to*** you ***for*** your help.
353) A residence of eight years in Sri Lanka had ***inured*** his system ***to*** the tropical climate.
354) We had ***resolved to make*** an early start.

❑ And thus, accede, adhere, allot, allude, apologize, appoint, ascribe, aspire, assent, attend, attribute, belong, conform, consent, contribute, lead, listen, object, occur, prefer, pretend, refer, revert, stoop, succumb, surrender, testify, yield, etc.— all the verbs take ***'to'*** *preposition* after them.

355) She decided to ***accede to*** the committee's request for more research.
356) It's important to ***adhere to*** the guidelines to ensure safety.
357) The manager will ***allot time to*** each team for their presentations.
358) In her speech, she managed to ***allude to*** the recent controversies without naming anyone.
359) He was quick to ***apologize to*** her for being late.
360) The board will ***appoint*** a new chairperson ***to*** lead the organization.
361) Many scientists ***ascribe to*** the theory that climate change is accelerated by human activity.
362) She ***aspires to*** become a renowned author one day.
363) The shareholders were quick to ***assent to*** the proposed changes.
364) It's crucial to ***attend to*** customer complaints promptly.
365) The success of the project can be ***attributed to*** the team's dedication.
366) These books ***belong to*** the library and must not be removed.
367) All products must ***conform to*** safety standards.

368) He gave his ***consent to*** the terms of the agreement.
369) Everyone is encouraged to ***contribute to*** the discussion.
370) His research could ***lead to*** significant advancements in technology.
371) Always take the time to ***listen to*** others' opinions.
372) She will ***object to*** the proposed changes during the meeting.
373) It never ***occurred to*** him that he might be wrong.
374) I ***prefer to*** travel by train rather than by plane.
375) The children love to ***pretend to*** be superheroes during playtime.
376) Please ***refer to*** the instructions for further details.
377) If the changes don't work, we might ***revert to*** the original plan.
378) He would never ***stoop to*** gossiping about others.
379) Many people ***succumb to*** temptation during the holiday season.
380) They decided to ***surrender to*** the inevitable and accept the outcome.
381) She was called to ***testify to*** the events she witnessed.
382) It's wise to ***yield to*** traffic laws when driving.

B. The Certain ***Verbs*** which are in most cases followed by the Preposition ***'from'***

383) ***Abstain from*** drinking & smoking. They are injurious to health.
384) The income ***derived from*** land ownership is commonly referred to as rent.
385) The two books ***differ*** greatly ***from*** each other.
386) Suddenly, it ***emerged from*** the cave & howled to startle all of us.
387) He ***escaped from*** jail, but within hours, he was sent back.
388) It is ***excluded from*** the list. ***Preserve*** it ***from*** rotting.
389) The noise from downstairs ***prevented*** me ***from*** sleeping.
390) Please ***protect*** us ***from*** their attack.
391) She ***recoiled from*** their touch and ran quickly, leaving them far behind.
392) He has been ***recovering from*** a fever for five days.
393) Learn to ***refrain from*** the bad company.

- And thus, alight, differ, prohibit, cease, defend, distinguish, divert, excuse, exempt, issue, emit, suffer, vary, etc. — all the verbs generally take ***'from'*** preposition after them.

394) The passengers will ***alight from*** the bus at the next stop.
395) Your opinion may ***differ from*** mine, but that's what makes discussions interesting.
396) The rules ***prohibit*** bringing food into the auditorium. (*does not take 'from'*)
397) Non-invitees are ***prohibited from*** entering the ceremony hall without permission.
398) The factory had to ***cease*** operations due to safety violations. (*does*

*not take 'from'*)

399) The lawyer will ***defend from*** any accusations made against her client.

400) It's important to ***distinguish between*** genuine feedback and mere criticism. (*take 'between'*)

401) It is ***distinguished from*** others.

402) We had to ****divert from**** our original route due to road construction.

403) She received an ****excuse from**** her teacher for missing class due to illness.

404) Certain students are ****exempt from**** taking the final exam if they meet specific criteria.

405) An important announcement will ****issue from**** the conference at noon.

406) The factory is required to monitor gases that ****emit from**** its smokestacks.

407) Many people ****suffer from**** chronic stress due to demanding jobs.

408) The results may ****vary from**** experiment to experiment based on several factors.

## Verbs with 'with', 'of', and 'about.'

C. The Certain ***Verbs*** which are in most cases followed by the Preposition ***'with'***

409) The new rules ***apply to*** all employees within the company.

410) I always ***associate*** the smell of baking ***with*** my childhood days.

411) He is closely ***associated*** in the public mind ***with*** his horror movies.

412) I ***associate*** myself ***with*** his remarks. (Agree with)

(John was an ***associate*** professor ***at*** Harvard University.)

413) The holy tree is ***associated with*** scenes of goodwill & rejoicing.

414) Her later work does not bear ***comparison with*** her earlier novels.

415) The supporters of two leading political parties ***clashed with*** each other.

416) The leaders ***clashed with*** the party members on the issue.

417) The strike ***coincided with*** the party conference.

418) Her story ***coincided*** exactly ***with*** her brother's.

419) They refused to ***comply with*** the new resolution.

420) He was ***endowed with*** gifts fitted to win eminence in any field of human activity. She ***persevered with*** her violin lesson.

- ❑ And thus, condole, cope, correspond, credit, deluge, differ, disagree, dispense, expostulate, fill, grapple, intrigue, meddle, part, quarrel, remonstrate, side, sympathize, trifle, vie, etc.— all the above verbs take

***'with'*** preposition after them.

421) I want to ***condole with*** you on the loss of your beloved pet.
422) I want to extend my ***condolences to*** you on the loss of your beloved pet. (when used as a noun)
423) She learned to ***cope with*** her stress through meditation and exercise.
424) He hopes to ***correspond with*** his pen pal regularly to improve his language skills.
425) The scientist was ***credited with*** discovering a new treatment for the disease.
426) The charity was ***deluged with*** donations after the disaster struck.
427) I often ***differ with*** my colleagues on the best approach to solving problems.
428) It's okay to ***disagree with*** someone, but it's important to remain respectful.
429) We decided to ***dispense with*** formalities and get straight to the meeting.
430) She felt the need to ***expostulate with*** her friend about the dangerous choices he was making.
431) The surprise party is sure to ***fill*** *her* ***with*** joy and excitement.
432) He continues to ***grapple with*** the complexities of the new project.
433) The mystery novel ***intrigued me with*** its unexpected twists and turns.
434) I would advise you not to ***meddle with*** things you don't understand.
435) It's hard for her to ***part with*** old, sentimental items she's collected over the years.
436) They often ***quarrel with*** each other but make up quickly after.
437) The teacher chose to ***remonstrate with*** the student about his disruptive behavior in class.
438) I tend to ***side with*** those who advocate for environmental protection.
439) I ***sympathize with*** her struggles, as I have faced similar challenges.
440) Don't ***trifle with*** her feelings; she deserves to be treated with respect.
441) The teams **vie with** each other for the championship title every year.

D. The Certain ***Verbs,*** which are in most cases followed by the Preposition ***'of /about.'***

442) The convict is finally ***acquitted of*** all charges against him.
443) ***Beware of*** coming danger and take steps accordingly.
444) She ***boasts of*** beauty and doesn't know it; she never lives long.
445) A man who always ***connives at*** the faults ***of*** his children is their worst enemy.
446) He ***died of*** a superman. The officer ***disapproved of*** all.
447) The writer is ***enamored of*** the subject.
448) He ***healed from*** injury and enlisted his name as a participant.

449) Everyone must ***repent of*** his or her ill-doings one day.

- And thus, despair, dispose, dream, judge, taste, etc.— all the above verbs take the ***'of'*** *preposition* after them.

450) It is *essential to* ***dispose of*** hazardous waste responsibly to protect the environment.

451) He often ***dreams of*** traveling the world, exploring new cultures and landscapes.

452) A true ***judge of*** character will see beyond appearances and understand a person's true nature.

453) The ***taste of*** homemade pasta is far *superior to* anything in a store.

## Verbs with 'for,' 'in,' and 'into.'

E. The Certain ***Verbs*** which are in most cases followed by Prepositions ***'for'***

454) Should you not ***atone for*** your crime?

455) He spent the whole month ***canvassing for*** votes.

456) People began to ***clamor for*** his resignation.

457) He ***hoped for*** none, and she went away alone.

458) The lady ***mourned for*** her husband's death, and while alive, she had only quarreled.

459) She ***pined for*** months after he'd gone. I feel ***sorry for*** him.

460) We ***started for*** Kolkata and reached after ten hours only.

461) We ***stipulated*** everything ***for*** the execution long before.

462) Ravi ***sued*** Rakesh ***for*** the breach of contract made between them.

463) We were eagerly ***waiting for*** our results, and the MBA results were declared postponed.

464) It is natural for every man to ***wish for*** distinction.

465) He ***yearns for*** nothing.

466) The President ***called for*** an immediate ***cessation of*** hostilities among the communities in West India.

F. The following **verbs** take the preposition ***'in'*** and ***'into'*** after them:

467) Isabella ***excelled in*** her unique performance on the stage.

468) She has never been one to ***indulge in*** gossip.

469) She was free to ***indulge in*** a little romantic daydreaming.

470) She was ***involved in*** the publication of the book.

471) How many vehicles were ***involved in*** the crash?

472) You have ***involved*** me ***in*** a great deal of extra work.

473) She would be ***engrossed in*** listening to the news on the TV.

474) The cat appears to have ***originated in*** Egypt or the East.

475) She ***persisted in*** her search for the truth.
476) Why do you ***persist in*** blaming yourself for what happened?
477) He ***persisted with*** his questioning.
478) His name was ***enlisted in*** the panel for recruitment.
479) In the classical age, the ideal life of Hindus was ***divided into*** four stages of ashrams.
480) The sound of his telephone ***intruded into*** his dream.

## Verbs with 'on, 'over, 'from,' and 'by'

G. The following **verbs** take the preposition ***'on,' 'over,' 'from,'*** or ***'by'*** after them:

481) Don't ***comment on*** others; look to yourself.
482) Who ***depends on*** you at home?
483) You made a mistake, but there is no need to ***dwell on*** it.
484) She didn't want to ***impose*** her values ***on*** her family.
485) A new tax was ***imposed on*** fuel.
486) He ***insisted on*** his innocence. (He insisted that he was innocent)
487) The government is ***trampling on*** the views of ordinary people.
488) Don't ***trample on*** the flowers.
489) The goat ***subsists on*** the coarsest of food.
490) Old people often ***subsist on*** minimal incomes.
491) She wouldn't let him ***trample over*** her any longer.
492) I ***differ from*** him ***on*** this point.
493) Alexander ***profited from*** the contentions of the Punjab Rajas.
494) ***Judged by*** its results, Hastings' policy was eminently successful.

## Exercise

2. Exercise-3: **Pick out Prepositions & also their objects**:

1) A black cat sat in the corner of a room.
2) Mrs. Persome asked Mary about the silver candlesticks.
3) There's no going home till morning if this weather lasts.
4) Humpty Dumpty sat on a wall.
5) The boy runs across the road.
6) The traveler slept in the woods beneath a large tree.
7) The dog overturned the burning candle onto the table.
8) You must discuss this matter with me.
9) Owing to acute hunger, the man began to eat the leaves of the trees.
10) They rise with the morning lark and labor till dark.
11) My grandmother sat by the window, looked out & told us ghost tales.

Answers to Exercise 3: **Pick out Prepositions & and their objects**

1) A black cat sat **in** *the corner* of a room.
2) Mrs. Persome asked Mary **about** *the silver candlesticks*.
3) There's no going home **till** *morning* if this weather lasts.
4) Humpty Dumpty sat **on** *a wall*.
5) The boy runs **across** *the road*.
6) The traveler slept in the woods **beneath** *a large tree*.
7) The dog overturned the burning candle **onto** *the table*.
8) You must discuss this **matter with** *me*.
9) Owing to acute hunger, the man began to eat the leaves **of** *the trees*.
10) They rise with the morning lark and labor **till** *dark*.
11) My grandmother sat **by** *the window*, looked out & told us ghost tales.

(The bold-lettered words are the prepositions when the underlined ones are their objects, objects to the prepositions)

3. Exercise 4: **Fill in the blanks with appropriate Prepositions**:
   a) He was born ____ a small town ____the district of Dakshin Dinajpur.
   b) We started ______ 5 o'clock ____ the morning.
   c) Distribute this _______ Om & Nicky.
   d) He refused to take less _____fifteen rupees for the soap.
   e) Here is the book that you asked _______.
   f) Who is the person you are speaking ______?
   g) Distribute the mangoes ______the boys.
   h) She wants to start ____seven o'clock in the morning.
   i) She has been there ______ three o'clock ____ the afternoon.
   j) It has been raining _____ two days.
   k) The girl has been suffering _____ $12^{th}$ instant.
   l) She began to write poems _____his boyhood.
   m) He will be in the office _______tomorrow.
   n) I didn't see Mr. Lahiri ____________three days.
   o) Here is a chair to sit ___________.
   p) The man has a reputation _______honesty. He has the reputation ______being a good policeman.
   q) She fell victim _______ cholera. The victims _____cholera were immediately sent to a hospital.
   r) He supplied cloths _____the poor. The poor were supplied ______the cloths
   s) We talk ____literature. They talk ______something else. I shall talk ____my daughter ____her attendance in college.
   t) The boy is negligent ____whatever he does. He is also negligent _____his duties.

4. Exercise 5: **Distinguish the prepositions from adverbs in the following sentences**:

1) Come down. (as an adverb)
2) We sailed down the river. (as a preposition)
3) The man walked around the house. (as a preposition)
4) He sat on a stool. (as a preposition)
5) The carriage moved on. (as an adverb)
6) The soldiers passed by. (as an adverb)
7) The man turned round. (as an adverb)
8) We all went in. (as an adverb)
9) He is in the room. (as a preposition)
10) He hid behind the door. (as a preposition)
11) I left him behind. (as an adverb)
12) She sat by the cottage door. (as a preposition)
13) The path leads through the woods. (as a preposition)
14) I have read the book through. (as an adverb)
15) The storm is raging without. (as an adverb)
16) We cannot live without water. (as a preposition)

## About Author

Mr. Peter is a professional teacher and author of numerous academic books on English Grammar and Writing Skills. Additionally, he has authored various works, including stories, novels, and poems in his original name. Mr. Peter's books have been published through global platforms such as Amazon and Notion Press.com, and these books are available in various formats, including e-books, audiobooks, Paperbacks, and Hardcovers, on different Amazon markets, as well as on Amazon Kindle, Notion Press.com, Google Play Store, and Google Books.
To locate his works, one can search by the book title or the author's name on the web browsers and platforms mentioned.
Thank you—best of Luck.

**Some important works by the writer & Co-author:**

1. Study of Nouns, Pronouns, Adjectives & Articles (detail study) ISBN: 979-832-697-263-7 / 979-832-697-510-2
2. All about Verbs (Forms, Functions, Conjugation, Tense, Voice Change, Forming Questions & Negation) ISBN: 979-832-807-531-2 / 979-832-807-688-3
3. Study of Adverbs, Prepositions, Conjunctions & Interjections ISBN: 979-832-886-943-0 / 979-883-987-196-0
4. Detail Study of Phrases, Clauses & Sentences, including Idioms & Phrasal Verbs ISBN: 979-832-939-104-6 / 979-884-011-097-3
5. Study of Subject-Verb Agreement, Narration Change, and Use of Punctuation, including Analysis, Synthesis, & Split-up (Study through charts, division, explanation, and examples) ISBN: 979-880-723-013-3 / 979-888-704-674-7
6. **Peter's 'English Grammar, A Complete Version of English Grammar,** (detail study, explanation & examples)ISBN: 979-879-725-020-3 / 979-888-704-463-7
7. **Question Bank of English Grammar & Composition**(Learn through Exercises) ISBN: 979-883-531-890-2 / 979-888-733-132-4
8. **Rhetoric & Prosody**(A handbook of Figures of Speech, rhymes, feet of poetic lines for High School Students) ISBN: 979-840-526-645-9 / 979-888-684-952-3
9. **A Book of Advanced Writing Skill, the Complete Version**(incl Part-1, 2 & 3) ISBN: 979-836-472-826-5 / 979-888-869-835-8
10. **English *Grammar* & Question Bank Together** For Class VI to XII (Learn through Exercise) ISBN 979-838-571-382-0
11. **New English Pal,** Class **10** (A Complete Guide Book for Smart Learning, based on WBBSE syllabus) by **P. Sarkar, based on Peter's Grammar and Composition**: [Separate book for each class from 5 to 10]
12. **The Rainbow** (A Collection of Short Stories) ISBN 10: 979-832141310-4; 979-832141545-0 & ISBN 13: 979-889363024-4

Author page URLs:
https://www.amazon.com/author/mr.peter
https://www.amazon.in/~/e/B09QW2P4TY(Bharat/India)
https://www.amazon.co.uk/~/e/B09QW2P4TY
https://www.amazon.de/~/e/B09QW2P4TY
https://www.amazon.fr/~/e/B09QW2P4TY
https://www.amazon.co.jp/~/e/B09QW2P4TY
https://www.amazon.es/~/e/B09QW2P4TY
https://www.amazon.it/~/e/B09QW2P4TY
https://www.amazon.com.br/kindle-dbs/entity/author?asin=B09QW2P4TY

In India, one can purchase the paperback and hardcover versions of his books by visiting notionpress.com or Amazon, and typing the author's name or the book title in the search box. They may also use these links:
https://www.facebook.com/groups/mr.peter,
https://notionpress.com/store/s?NP_Books%5Bquery%5D=Mr.+Peter,
https://notionpress.com/store/s?NP_Books%5Bquery%5D=P.+Sarkar.

The Following Coupons can be applied on **notionpress.com** till the end of the coupons:

| ***Coupon Codes*** | **Book Name** | **Buy for** | **Discount %** | **Rebate Prices** |
|---|---|---|---|---|
| ~~PujaDeal1 / Deal1~~ | Study of Nouns, Pronouns, Adjectives & Articles (detail study) | ~~1 & more~~ | ~~20 & 26~~ | ~~280 224 & 208~~ |
| PujaDeal2 / Deal2 | All about Verbs (Forms, Functions, Conjugation, Tense, Voice Change, Forming Questions & Negation) | 1 & more | 18 & 26 | ~~420~~ 345 & 311 |
| PujaDeal3 / Deal3 | Study of Adverbs, Prepositions, Conjunctions & Interjections | 1 & more | 20 & 26 | ~~260~~ 208 & 193 |
| PujaDeal4 / Deal4 | Detail Study of Phrases, Clauses & Sentences, including Idioms & Phrasal Verbs | 1 & more | 20 & 26 | ~~290~~ 232 & 215 |
| PujaDeal5 / Deal5 | Study of Subject-Verb Agreement, Narration Change, Use of Punctuation, including Analysis, Synthesis & Split-up | 1 & more | 20 & 26 | ~~301~~ 241 & 223 |
| PujaDeal6 / Deal7 | Question Bank of English Grammar & Composition | 1 & more | 20 & 28 | ~~559~~ 448 & 403 |
| PujaDeal7 / Deal8/ bulk11 | Rhetoric & Prosody | 1 & more | 20, 26 & 55 | ~~240~~ 192, 178 &108 |
| PujaDeal8 / Deal9 | Steps to Composition (Development of Writing Skill, from Primary to Secondary Level, Part-1) | 1 & more | 20 & 26 | ~~300~~ 240 & 222 |
| PujaDeal9 / Deal10 | Development of Writing Skill, Part 2 | 1 & more | 18 & 24 | ~~365~~ 300 & 278 |
| PujaDeal10 / Deal11 | Development of Writing Skill, Part 3 | 1 & more | 18 & 24 | ~~365~~ 300 & 278 |
| unique00 / bulk00 | A Book of Advanced Writing Skills, the Complete Version (incl. Part-1, 2 & 3) | 1 & more | 15 & 23 | ~~780~~ 663 & 601 |
| unique01 / bulk1/bulk10 | Peter's 'English Grammar' (Complete Version of English Grammar) | 1 & more | 23, 30 & 48 | ~~1201~~ 925, 841 & 625 |
| ~~unique02/bulk03~~ | English Grammar & Question Bank Together | 1 & more | 30 | 590 |
| spl01 / bulk04 | New English Pal, Class 9 (based on WBBSE syllabus) | 1 & more | 35 & 47 | ~~490~~ 319 & 260 |
| spl02 / bulk05 | New English Pal, Class 10 (based on WBBSE syllabus) | 1 & more | 34 & 47 | ~~480~~ 317 & 255 |
| spl03 / bulk06 | New English Pal, Class 5 (based on WBBSE syllabus) | 1 & more | 29 & 52 | ~~280~~ 199 & 134 |
| spl04 / bulk07 | New English Pal, Class 8 (based on WBBSE syllabus) | 1 & more | 30 & 46 | ~~420~~ 294 & 227 |
| spl05 / bulk08 | New English Pal, Class 7 (based on WBBSE syllabus) | 1 & more | 30 & 54 | ~~400~~ 280 & 184 |
| spl06 / bulk09 | New English Pal, Class 6 (based on WBBSE syllabus) | 1 & more | 30 & 56 | ~~320~~ 224 & 141 |
| spl07 / bulk12 | The Rainbow (A Collection of Short Stories) | 1 & more | 56 & 56 | ~~299~~ 132 & 132 |
| Note: For Copies of More Than One, Select The 2nd Coupon Given in Each Row of The First Column | | | | |

www.ingramcontent.com/pod-product-compliance
Ingram Content Group UK Ltd.
Pitfield, Milton Keynes, MK11 3LW, UK
UKHW062308290726
14090UKWH00018B/949